Digital M...

Attract The Clients You *Really* Want

And Grow Your Business <u>Fast</u>

Ben Waters

Published by
Digital Magnet Ltd
www.Digital-Magnet.uk

Second Edition published 2016

What others are saying...

"This is a clear and concise book that not only explains why we should market our products and/or services but importantly explains in an understandable way why it is crucial that we market our products and/or services in the correct way

:i.e. The 3 M's. Market Message Medium – Know our market, use the right message and use the right medium to get that message to the right market. It sounds simple but there is a reason why so many of us get it wrong and this book shows us how to Attract the Right Clients."

 **Fergal McCarthy FCCA ATT(Fellow)**
M3 Evolve
www.m3evolve.com

M3 Evolve provide accountancy, tax planning and business growth advice to Clients in Essex/London.

"I must say that it was a very interesting read which has encouraged us to re-think the way that we work and do business. Sometimes, we all need to be given an alternative view in order to move our business forward and for us, this was it."

Steve Lowery
Think Business Support
www.thinkbs.co.uk

Think Business Support provide commercial cleaning, estate / property management services and much more. Think Business Support utilise a comprehensive bespoke maintenance platform to ensure jobs are serviced quickly and efficiently.

"I found this book really informative, which has left me with a clear goal…to completely re-do our online marketing. It's easy to read, and it's pretty clear that if you follow the outlined ideas and strategies, you're going to do well out of it – I know I'm confident we will great results from this."

John Galley
Kestrel Printing
www.kestrel-printing.co.uk

Kestrel Printing provide a wide range of print services, from the basics of business cards to brochures or any large format printing.

"I have read through with increasing interest. Having identified many of my traits, I discovered that my world of problems and insurmountable hurdles are pretty much everyone's. I am not alone!! That's a start. Given how different each business is I easily identified many tips and tests that I can (and will) use to measure and grade the results of my efforts and improve the progress of my business.

"What becomes clear too, is that the more structured your efforts, the less time, effort and money is wasted so clear and efficient strategies can be formed. The book provides you with the shopping list of tools to build that strategy. Your examples help to choose which ones to pick off the shelf.

"There are many business guru's out there and I liked that you have used, tested and commented on many proven ideas and formulas. Each chapter is thus leaving me with the best of breed to choose more easily the most appropriate for my business."

Colin Merenda
Merenda Insurance
www.merenda.co.uk

Merenda Insurance provide peace of mind by ensuring you've got the right cover at the right price. If it comes to making a claim, Merenda take the stress out of it all by acting as an intermediary between you and the insurance company. From business insurance to car insurance, if you need it covered – Merenda can help.

"Ben Waters is someone rather unusual in the business and marketing world.

"For a start, he knows what he's talking about. As a man in business himself he knows just how damn hard things can be sometimes, and what it really takes to succeed. I can't help but feel that in some ways he's made his life even more difficult, because not only does he have to grow his own business but since his business is helping other businesses succeed (particularly through pay-per-click marketing) he has to deliver results for them too.

"You can't do that if you don't know your stuff.

"The second thing that separates Ben from almost everyone else out there is that he tells it like it is. No sugar-coating, no bullshit, no airy fairy "branding" crap - just practical ways to deliver results.

"So if you want to grow your business and appreciate straight talking from someone who's actually been there and done it...

"...then buy this book.

"It could be the best business investment you make this year."

Dr. Dev Lall FRCS
www.privatepracticeexpert.co.uk

Contents

Preface

This book, my second edition, is largely the same 'principle' as my first book but I have added, modified and removed huge chunks of content.

There's a lot of truths in this book, which you might find uncomfortable and you might not like that. Also, there's going to be the odd swear word; if bad language offends you, you might want to put this book back down.

And that's fine... if you don't want to grow your business enough to go through a little discomfort, or you simply plain disagree with what I'm saying, then let me know and I'll give you a full refund. If you didn't buy from me direct just send me a copy of the receipt; I'll refund whatever you paid (and you can even keep the book.)

There's a reason for me saying this to you here; I want you to understand that this book has some seriously powerful information and techniques which *will* help you grow your business if you put them to work - but you can't come into this with a closed mind.

You have to accept that you're reading this book for a reason: you want change. Right? If you don't want change (i.e. more income, more free time, etc) then this book probably isn't for you.

Something that you'll come to understand, as you read this book, is that you're not for everyone. If you try to be everything to everyone you end up being the exact opposite: nothing. I know *I'm* not for everyone, for sure... So that's why I offer my Guarantee; love this book, or get a full refund.

Now, getting to what's *actually in this book* - it's a common myth that you will be successful if you simply work hard and get some luck.

Whilst I've seen that attitude work with a handful of business owners, I've also seen hard working business owners fail time and time again because they essentially burnt themselves out working too hard.

And it's not fair to say that you "need" luck to be successful; anyone can create their own success, it just comes down to how much work you want to put in and *how* and *what* you actually do.

(Here's a spoiler: I'm not about working 18 hours a day and never seeing the family. I hate the term "work smarter, not harder" but it's pretty much what you have to do).

What I'm really saying is, that as much as you might believe when you look at some business owners out there - it's not about luck. Now quite obviously, having a good bit of luck can't and won't hurt but in the most part - it's simply about working smart, and working hard.

I'm not saying you should work ridiculous hours either; I've *been through* the 18 hour days, to come out the other side realising it made me no more money than if I worked 8.

Sure… in the *short term*, for maybe a few weeks or even few months, working 18 hour days can be really profitable. You can fit a shit load of work into that time, and if you're "swapping time for money" then it makes sense.

But there's a finite limit before you start to get worn down; you start to resent the clients, the work, and anyone around the business.

I got to the stage of resenting my workforce, because they were only working a fraction of the hours I was, yet on some months earned more than I did.

Working *more hours* isn't the answer. The more rested you are, the more charged and in love with your business you are, the more committed you'll be when you actually need to *do the work.*

You won't sit on Facebook; you won't check Skype; you won't sit around chatting about X Factor or whatever rubbish TV is worth talking about.

You'll be focused, driven and getting on with the work you need to get on with that directly results in business growth.

Trust me when I say that you might be the best plumber in town, but none of that matters if you don't take one thing into consideration. How you market yourself, your business and your positioning.

Your 'positioning' refers to how you place yourself in the market, i.e. If you're seen as offering 'cheap' then you'll attract only those that want to pay cheap.

Marketing can be really hard work, and subsequently many people overlook it, or think they can get away with just focusing on one strategy such as referrals or advertising in the local paper.

But the thing is, Marketing is largely just about implementation. Implementing ideas and measuring the results, and *learning from those results*.

So if you were to take just one thing away from this book (and I'd like you to take a lot more), please take 'implementation' as the key message.

If you don't implement anything, if you don't try different marketing techniques, and just rely on that word of mouth or that standard advert in the paper – you're not only losing out to the competition, but more importantly you're risking the stability of your business.

"I don't have time to do all this Marketing *stuff"*

I know that feeling. I know the feeling that if you stop what you're doing you're not going to get the cash in the door, it's a real catch-22 situation.

For *years* I took the wrong attitude in running my business, I took the attitude that I should be the one doing the main work. That is to say, it took me many years to realise I had not created a business, but a job for myself and that's exactly what left me in the catch-22 situation.

In fact even when this was pointed out to me (not directly, but at a training event) and I thought I'd made enough changes - really, nothing had changed. I kept on doing the same things in reality, with the excuse of "but if I don't do that it won't get done, and we need that to get the next payment through the door".

The reason for this was primarily cash flow. Cash flow is, as you know, the thing that pretty much dictates what you do.

Or at least it *was* for me at that time. My point is I felt couldn't afford to stop doing the work and delegate/outsource because then I wouldn't have enough money in the bank to pay the bills.

At some point in the last few years, and I can't really pinpoint the exact time it happened, I realised I had to stop focusing on the money and focus on my actions instead.

What transpired eventually was a kind of emotional detachment from the money; what I mean by that is previously I'd be obsessing over winning the contract because of the financial figure. When you take the financial element out of a contract, deciding whether you want to do it or not becomes far more important.

This allows you to be far more objective over delivering a proposal (note: you should call a proposal an *action plan*, not a proposal) or promoting your product/service via a marketing piece etc. And if a client attempts to negotiate on price, you know you don't have to bow down to the pressure because you don't care about the money.

Returning to the point in hand, are you feeling like you've got to be working 24/7 to be earning the cash, rather than stopping and breathing for a moment, and reflecting on what *marketing* you can do?

Well, you simply have to be sensible about things. Understand that an hour here or an hour there won't stop you from paying your mortgage, but it quite possibly would help you win a contract 5x the size you normally get.

And by winning a contract 5x the size you normally would get, you start to remove that constant pressure on you to be foraging around for work/clients. It allows you to breathe and get on with what you need to get on with: focusing on your Marketing.

Don't get me wrong, you can't be stupid about this and just instantly take off 3 weeks to focus on your Marketing. (I have done that, and it really caused me a *lot* of problems).

But, by focusing things I'll go into in this book - which have been inspired by some great people - you'll be able to introduce implementation in a way that grows your business. And fast.

Now I don't consider my book to have all the answers, but what it *does* have is many guidelines and principles that if you adhere to them, will result in your business becoming far more successful.

Off the back of these strategies, I have developed a successful Web Design and Marketing Business that is rapidly becoming less and less dependent on me on a daily basis and steadily and rapidly increasing turnover and profitability.

And that's the Holy Grail here because the less you're tied up doing the day to day operational bits - the more time you've got to focus on the Marketing and growing of your Business.

CHAPTER ONE

Introduction

What Do You Want?

So before we actually get going on any of these strategies, before you actually get knee deep in marketing: what's your goal?

What do you want? Where do you want to be in 3 years? Is it a financial goal? Or perhaps just to have your business being independent from you.

I'll come back to the business dependency in a minute, but first I want to focus on your mindset. Without the right focus, without the right goals in mind and without wanting to *actually achieve* those goals, you're not going to progress any further than where you are now.

Also, and this is hugely important, finding a goal setting strategy that works with your personality is incredibly important.

I've worked with a number of business coaches and mentors over the years, and they've all had various strategies and methods for growing your business.

The thing is, many of them are so 'wrong' for my personality that it's a wonder (actually, it isn't, as you'll see in a second) I even began a conversation with them in the first place, let alone paid them ridiculous sums of money.

As a business owner, I'm not afraid of taking risks, and I'm pretty impulsive. I'm extremely logical (I guess a benefit of being a programmer?) so if I can see clear benefits outweighing disadvantages I won't hang around in making a decision. I'll give it a try.

If the outcome is completely unknown, but the potential reward is higher than the potential risk, I won't even think twice.

As I say, impulsive. And that's not a bad thing, if handled correctly. If you sit me down and try and make me manage spreadsheets of financial data, or work on the business from a purely technical point of view, you're in for a whole lot of bad language.

My point here is, you've got to find a way of growing your business that revolves around the sort of person you are: don't let people try and change your core personality.

Sure, you've probably got to make some changes to grow your business, and you'll have to go through some 'uncomfortable' change, but that's not to say you have to sacrifice what makes you 'you'.

Now, what are the key elements of a successful business? What should we be aiming for?

You know, many small business owners I have talked to over the years, haven't really been small business owners at all. Even if they've got ten staff, if the business is *completely dependent* on their actions, they've created a company with a job for themselves. Now if you've got ten staff it's a lot easier to start removing yourself from the business than if you've got just one, but my point is: your business should not *depend* on you on a daily basis.

If you walk away from your Business for four, eight or even twelve weeks, will it still be running (fine) by the time you get back?

The other key to running a successful business is to ensure you've got a completely automated marketing process. Quite often, when I'm talking to clients about marketing for the first time, they seem to doubt it's possible to have an automated process to the point of just delivering them leads that are more than just leads - they're practically sales waiting for you to just take their money.

It's easy to make this sound like a "magic pill" and for it to sound like I can help you wave a magic wand - I want to be clear - it's not *that* easy - but it *is* possible to have a system like this.

In a lead generation system, with an email auto-responder you can create the perfect system that sends emails over the course of 2-3 months, runs Webinars, sends sales letters, schedules phone calls, etc.

There are many systems you can use that give you this sort of functionality, I use a combination of many. I also make use of a company to send out letters on my behalf, meaning I don't have to touch anything until it comes to the scheduled phone call.

So if you've got a business that's not dependent on you, and that's got an automated marketing system, is that enough? Almost... the rest comes down to good staff.

Now whilst I can give some advice on years of hiring and firing, the core of this comes down to finding the people that enjoy working for you. That means, just like your marketing, you have to attract employees that are like *you* personality-wise, and you've got to reward them relative to their performance.

So with all that in mind, what's your goal? To get your business independent from you? To build an automated marketing system? To find the right employee?

In The Right Mindset...

Back when I first started getting serious about my business, I started exploring the 'business mentors' out there. I was recommended one in particular by someone a friend.

The person I was referred to was one of the leading 'info marketers' out there. That is to say, his business is to provide information on how to market your business.

There was a particular marketing product, which was a series of telephone seminars etc. - and this was probably my first exposure to the word 'marketing'.

Until that point I had simply thought of marketing as advertising, but obviously it's just so much more than that.

Anyway, this marketer would run seminars and had all sorts of other products etc... so I thought I'd see what my friend was doing with their material, and if they were going to purchase anything else.

My friend had taken a *little* action, but the thing I noted was that he'd decided not to do anything else with the material, or buy any additional material on the basis that the all the marketer sells is sells is 'mindset'.

The marketer was someone I had started following pretty intensely, and having been in a mastermind group of this person, I can tell you that that's not the case *but* if you don't have the right mindset none of it will work, leading you to wonder what's gone wrong.

Without the right mindset, this whole book is useless to you. If you don't think certain things are going to be possible, your mind will argue with itself over every decision you take to improve your business, and subsequently you won't end up taking action on a lot of the things you *should* take action on.

So from the outset, we have to change our thinking. I have to tell you, for years, even listening to a lot of seriously successful Marketers and the like, I struggled.

The thing is, many of these Marketers out there, want to give you enough information to make a difference, because it keeps you coming back, but they don't really give you what you need to scale your business completely.

And that's because it's not easy to simply shift the way you approach your sales, marketing, and in fact, everything about your business. Changing my business for example, took more than changing my marketing.

My marketing, for the large part, over the latter few years, has had a very common theme. However the approach with which I run my business, has changed dramatically.

Throughout this book, you'll find other references to Marketers who have seriously influenced what I do, along with how I think.

Additionally, the one thing that truly helped me grow my business was focusing on *one* mentor. You see, I simultaneously was in a high end mastermind group *and* had a business coach *and* was listening to at least two other marketers for advice.

The problem with that is you get conflicting levels of importance on various aspects of your business or marketing, and the conflict ends up driving a wedge between you and the business.

This actually ended up in the destruction of my cashflow, whereby I was so consumed with trying to follow the advice of multiple mentors I essentially 'took my eye off the ball' and brought myself to a crashing halt with no sales and no income. This is easily fixed, of course, if you're able to just focus on the single most important thing: getting in sales at the right price from the right people.

So to build your business you have to accept you have to learn; you almost certainly have to 'change' and, referencing my earlier point, you can't change your core personality but you probably need to instigate changes in your working life.

As a prime example of that, one of the changes I made in my life relatively recently, was to start getting up ridiculously early (5am) and working from home for a couple of hours. That extra couple of hours made a huge difference to what I can get done in a week, and in fact is one of the ways I ended up writing this book.

Of course, it's not about making your day *longer*, it's about making use of your time better. So I take a break for the kids school run, and take a long lunch to hit the gym.

Now change isn't easy, and it comes down to a few things, the primary one of course being mindset and as I keep banging on about mindset, let's start by defining it.

Mindset is a set of assumptions, methods or notations held by one or more people, that is so established it creates a powerful incentive within this person/people that they continue to adopt or accept prior behaviours choices or tools.

That is to say you believe things are the way they are because that's the way they are and they can't be changed.

i.e. *That's* the software you've got to use, *that's* the only marketing platform you can use, the only way to get X done is by doing ABC etc.

A classic example of this is from my personal life relatively recently. I have used a Microsoft/Windows PC since around 1992 - right now, that's 24 years. So I have been obsessed by much of the latest Windows marketing including the tablets they provide, etc.

I loved using the hardware such as the Microsoft Surface, but I started to hit problems with both the software *and* the hardware. In fact, it would often just be a small problem, but add it up over the years and I've spent *vast* amounts of time dealing with problem after problem that's meant my PC has been slow or needed a reboot or something. Being frustrated, I would always just put it down to "that's the way it is".

More recently I'd have trouble with the operating system, freezing randomly on certain applications and causing me all sorts of headaches. Now, I'm not saying it's "Microsofts fault" - I'm not trying to dish out the blame or anything. I'm sure the latest version of Windows works really well, and millions upon millions of people are enjoying it… but in *my* setup, with what *I* needed it to do, it was causing *me* headaches.

But I had no choice, right? I have *always* used Windows and I could never use anything else.

That was my mindset. I *couldn't* change. Until one day the pain got so great, I thought, you know what? I'm going to *try*. I went out and bought a Macbook that afternoon (I might have also been in a slight rage at the time, having had a crash which was massively delaying me getting some work done). Since that day, almost a year later, I have been working faster than ever before, I haven't looked back.

That's not to say Apple are better than Microsoft - that's not my argument here, but for me, for what I want to do, in the way I want to do it, the Apple solution has been better. My mindset for *years* prevented me from grasping it fully. It prevented me from finding the 'Apple way' to do things, rather than just assuming it was inferior and the 'Windows way' was better (my Windows loving side still complains about many "features" of Apple - but the pain is mild compared to the stress I had before).

By accepting the mindset change, I transformed how much work I could get done, and subsequently I grew my business even faster. Something else happened too; because I got frustrated less with 'PC problems' I found my overall stress levels massively declined when it came to using the computer.

So you see, mindset is very important. A fixed mindset will stop you achieving a lot of things; it'll stop you changing your PC, your phone, your habits, but most importantly, your clients.

And it's your clients that you really, almost certainly, need to change. Sure, I don't know you or your business. I don't know your clients. But I know one thing: you're reading this book. That means you want a change of some sort right? And that's most likely going to come from the type of work you're doing or the type of people you're doing it for.

Accept just one thing for today: *something has to change*. Accept that, and you're on your way to creating the change you need to improve your business.

Sorry to break it to you...

So I'm sorry to break it to you (actually, I'm not really), but no-one cares about you. Apart from your significant other, your family, and perhaps close friends - no-one cares about you, your business, your logo, your brand, or pretty much anything you do.

OK, let's take an "average" business owner (if there is such a thing) and how they might think about advertising their business or Product/Service.

The first thing you're keen to do, especially if you've been in business a few years, is make sure your logo is nice and prominent, along with "Established X Years" or similar.

The issue here, is your 'headline', whether it be on your website or your printed advertising, is often your logo. However your headline should be something to *capture the readers attention* - or be directly related to the product/service they're after, or, better still, the *problem* that your product relates to/solves.

For example, if we're talking about offering a website, there are a whole host of problems that business owners face when it comes to sorting their online presence. Firstly, most web designers are focused on one thing: design. Secondly, many business owners don't realise the most important thing about a website is how it's marketed, not how it looks - subsequently they're not used to it generating business for them.

So you need to create a message which captures their attention by offering them something different: you need to offer them something they *want*.

This message must be carried throughout all of your marketing material, from everything in your brochures, to your website, your online video and even your ads. When you're speaking to potential customers you have to keep this at the forefront of your mind.

When they're *first* reading about your product/service, and I mean in the "initial" sales copy they're reading about you - your potential customers really don't care how long you've been in business, they don't need to be told about how great your product or service is, and the majority don't care about how much it costs.

There's quite a lot in that statement, so let's break it down... we have three main points to focus on here:

- They don't care how great your product/service is
- They don't care how long you've been in business
- They don't care how much it costs

You might be thinking "this is complete bullshit - of course they care about how good the product/service is".

Well, yes of course they do but these are things that are considered *standard*. They shouldn't have to be told your product is good quality in the initial sales copy, or that you have personal service, because these are things that you should be doing regardless and *don't* make you unique. When it comes to making a *decision* something that you must burn into your mind is:

"What's in it for me?"

It's this phrase that people are entirely focused on (mostly without conscious realisation) and subsequently means that they don't care how long you've been in business, and that the notion that people buy on price is wrong.

A small percentage of people *do* always buy on price, and will always look for the cheapest deal possible – but you want to avoid those people, because they will generally make your life hell. It's *always* the customers who want the cheapest deal that end up causing you the most aggravation.

You might realise you have customers like that already; what you won't realise at this stage is how sacking them as customers will make your life significantly better. I went through a stage of sacking nearly half my clients several years ago, and it was one of the best decisions I have made. Additionally, I put measures in place that meant I wouldn't get customers on board like them again, simply by positioning myself better (I'll cover positioning later on in the book).

The reality of it is, people buy *based on desire*; they buy something because it's going to make them feel good or solve a problem.

If all people bought on price, wouldn't *everyone* be driving the cheapest car?

Wouldn't *everyone* have a cheap Android phone instead of an iPhone?

Isn't it funny that when it comes to something they <u>*really*</u> want, they can 'find' the money? Perhaps that latest 50" TV just in time for the Football.

Think about smokers; they're people that really buy based on desire, on a regular basis. Some (a minority, obviously) have absolutely no money to speak of yet still, even when living on the edge of affordability in terms of paying their rent or keeping food on the table, will make sure they have enough tobacco to smoke.

It's plain and simple - we buy, based on desire. So remember this: your branding, your logo, and everything about you is irrelevant. What's important is: what can you do for your customer that benefits *them*.

People Want To Be Sold To

Now here's a funny thing... people often think that selling is a dirty word. They think that they're no good at sales because they don't want to harass people or offer them something they don't want.

Selling is much more than simply harassing people. Yes, it's about staying in touch, but it's not about offering them something they don't want or need, it's about finding what they need, then providing them with the route to getting it. The last thing I'd ever do is 'harass' someone, *but* I do believe in keeping in touch with people until they buy, die, or tell you to go away.

And in fact, even the latter, sometimes you want to persist because if you have a product or service that can significantly change your prospective clients life for the better, then (and I think it was Chet Holmes who said this) it's *your moral obligation* to ensure you provide it to them.

The thing is, people *want* to read about how your product/service will make their life better.

Whether it's a more comfortable pen to write with, or the most luxurious car, people *want* to be sold to. They want to read about how amazing it will be with this product in their life.

Once you master this process you'll find that your marketing material becomes all about how you can solve the customer's problems, and not about how you're here to help because you've been in business 25 years.

On that note, I'm not saying you should remove the fact that you've been in business 25 years either; on your website there are plenty of ways to build that in without directly injecting into the primary sales pitch. It's good to have history and even better if you've got awards or other qualifications.

These things belong primarily in the 'About Us' section of your website. That's what it's for. It's for about you, although having said that, if you write your 'About Us' content correctly, even everything that's about you can be everything about your potential customer. Just remember to focus on the problems of the reader, and how you solve them with your product/service.

Take this example: some time back, must be a few years now, I wrote up a postcard to send out to business owners. I had it critiqued by one of the biggest marketing names in the world.

My thought process behind the headline was to capture interest, essentially trying to get them to read the next line (which would promise to explain *why* they should read more).

The headline was:

"Do you know what Google Re-marketing is?"

And here's the feedback I got: Let's assume the reader doesn't know what Google Re-marketing is. The reader will almost certainly respond by saying to themselves "No, and I don't care" as they put it in the bin.

What would be a far more suitable headline, is a headline that speaks *to the problems* of that Business Owner.

"Do You Want To *Easily* Reach Customers Who Visited Your Website, But Left No Details?"

Immediately, you're changing the whole question. And in fact you could go on improving that by focusing on lost profits from not reaching these people etc.

But you're changing the focus, it's not about a technology issue, it's about reaching potential customers who are otherwise inaccessible to you.

You can follow the advert on then with sales copy that talks about how to generate more business by reaching potential customers who have visited your website, looked at particular products/information and *not* purchased *or* enquired.

Your content should follow a set number of rules (which are detailed later) – but most importantly, you must remember, your headline is there to get them to read the first line of your content, and whilst you might read a headline and think it's seriously compelling, and makes complete sense to you, you have to put yourself in your prospective customer's shoes.

That's a really hard thing to do, because for a large part you have to 'not care' about yourself or your company to get the right attitude. That's one reason getting your content critiqued by a third party can be hugely helpful.

So if the headline is there to get them to read the first line of content, the first line of your content is there to get them to read the second line of your content.

And the third line is… you get the idea. My point here is that you need to hook the reader on a headline that means something to them, and then be careful to focus.

I've been guilty of this before in fact; having a headline and main content that's not entirely unrelated, but that doesn't completely flow. Again, returning to having someone critique my work, I produced a landing page which I *thought* combined a series of powerful headlines.

The thing is, whilst the headlines were quite powerful, and all roughly related to what I wanted to sell, there wasn't enough 'flow' between it. If you like, it was almost cutting off mid-sentence and starting again.

And it's the flow that counts, because if your content flows, then the reader has got to the end (which should be the call to action) without even realising it.

CHAPTER TWO

The Essentials

The 80/20 Rule

So I'm about to introduce you to two numbers which genuinely changed my life. They changed my life for a number of reasons, actually.

They changed my life because I *applied* them. I didn't just read them and wonder how to implement them; I didn't just read about them and think "nice idea in theory but..." - I grasped hold of them and immediately started making changes.

I'm referring to the 80/20 rule. That rule dictates that 80% of your results come from 20% of your efforts; if you've ever had a business coach or mentor, the likelihood is you've heard this before. *How* they get you to apply it, varies wildly I have found.

Before I get too involved in how to apply it, let's cover the 80/20 rule a little more. Where did it come from? What is it?

Well, it's also referred to as the Pareto Principle, because it was discovered by an economist called

Wilfredo Pareto. He published his first paper at the end of the 19th Century, which showed that 80% of the land in Italy was owned by just 20% of the population. He carried out further surveys to discover that similar distribution applied to other countries, calculating that 20% of the world population controlled 80% of the World's income.

The rule just seems to apply to everything - however bizarre that may be. 20% of your carpet gets 80% of the wear, 20% of software features are used 80% of the time, etc.

Now, I find it has two main applications in business (you can apply it in your personal life too, but for now I'll focus on the business). Your client base and your time management.

One of the 'tricks' I tend to get people to do first, is to take a look at their sales over the last 3 years (or however long they've been trading if less than 3 years).

They then sort their clients by the amount of revenue they've generated from them. Take the top 20% and that's the list we work with; then, sort that list in 'how easy were they to deal with'?

Take the top 20% again. *That's* not only your ideal customer, i.e. The type of customer/business you want more of... but it's also a list of people for you to go back to, time and time again, to sell more to.

The 'sell' doesn't have to be much either; if they're your best customer financially and they're easy to deal with, you can just pick up the phone and ask them how they're doing, and that you're just keeping in touch to see if there's anything they need right now. You'll be amazed at how well that works (the first time you will, anyway, after that it'll become a routine).

You'll also find that you can do this on a regular basis; every 6 months or so you can go over your new clients, rate them in your 80/20 style, and keep offering your top 20% more services. The end result is your 20% expands more and more, until perhaps your top 20% is your top 40%.

This is a great way to grow your business because you're doing it based purely on people you enjoy working with (you're always modelling your 20% on the people you enjoy working with the most).

80/20 Time Management

So, what's one of the 'nicest' problems to have? It's the problem where you're getting too much business in, and you need to focus on delivery. This most likely depends on your time management, to ensure that you deliver on time.

I've had this problem quite a few times over the years, and until I sorted out my time management I always ended up in the same scenario: Feast or Famine.

I'd do a load of marketing, get a load of sales in, then spend the next few months trying to deliver, all the while not doing any more marketing (because I had too much work). I was celebrating, thinking I'd cracked this business lark, loads of cash in the bank but by the time I got to the end of the work - I'd run out of money and there was no work left to do, and no leads in the pipeline.

What can you do in a scenario like this except panic? I did, regularly. I'd sit at my desk with my head in my hands because I knew the solution - I needed to generate leads to generate the sales, but that needed cash (which I'd run out of). I'd fix it short term by taking out another loan or credit card to live off, planning to pay it off on the next 'big contract'. Only it never gave me enough to do so.

So I needed a good, long term solution to fix my feast or famine situation, which I think many business owners face (many I've spoken with, at least).

Well, if we look at time management from an 80/20 perspective, and we know that 80% of your profits will come from 20% of your efforts then that means 80% of what *you* do is not profitable.

It's not that it's a waste of time, and its not that you can ignore these tasks or skimp on the quality of them, in fact just the opposite, it's getting these tasks done to a high standard that keeps you delivering at a premium price - so whilst these jobs 'must be done' - they don't always have to be done **by you**.

Essentially what we're doing here is drilling down on what *you* do that makes you money, what's *your* key skill that makes your business generate the income it generates. Again, like doubling the 20% of your 'best' customers, we want to focus on doubling the 20% of your time that makes you money.

Now this process varies, but let's take something I'm pretty familiar with: a typical web design sale process. The typical process can have a couple of meetings, a sales phase, design phase, development, then content and finally the sign off when it's made live (this is assuming no real complications).

I was always forced to outsource *part* of this process, because for many years (I'm not *so* bad now with the years of experience behind me) I couldn't design. I openly admitted to my clients the one thing I couldn't ever do was create them a nice design, it's why I employed a designer. This had massive advantages for reasons which I'll come to later.

In the meantime, let's take our typical process:

- Enquiry comes in
- Initial discussion results in setting appointment
- Initial Consultation
- Creation of Specification
- Negotiation of Sale
- Creation of Design
- Modification/'Sign off' of Design
- Development of Design
- Integration of code into actual Website
- Implementation of content
- Setting up Hosting
- Bug Testing
- Hand over to client
- Final changes
- Sign off

Until I really grasped the 80/20 rule, I can say I was probably doing 80-90% of those tasks. Now it's less than 20%. Now, I'm not saying you should outsource everything just to off-load it from your schedule, but what I *am* saying is you should only be doing the things that essentially result in what the people are paying *you* for.

So, for example, I write the content, and I'm pretty active in orchestrating the design. Whilst I don't actually *do* design work, I understand direct response - something most web designers don't. I drill it in to those I work with so that it becomes easier, because people come to me for a direct response website and marketing campaign - so that's what I make sure they get.

I have met many business owners over the years, and many other web designers (who, unlike me, actually have the ability to 'design'). The greatest commonality with them all, is they are stuck on the "have to do everything" approach. The result is they get a lot of work and then just explode under the pressure.

The point here? Grasp 80/20, grasp delegation and outsourcing, and you'll have a more profitable and robust business.

So how do you actually implement 80/20 from a Time Management point of view?

Well, the way I did this (initially), was to get an A4 diary. You can do this on just paper, but I prefer using a diary. You can carry it around with you more easily and if you draw a line down the middle, you can use it for your scheduling as well as what you've been doing.

This method *needs some discipline* - you can't just half do it. It won't work. I confess, I failed at doing this many times before getting pissed off just one too many times that it wasn't working - and I stuck to it rigidly.

I recommend using a phone timer if you're one to easily lose track of time (I know I am). Depending on how good your memory is, choose a frequency appropriate to you. I think 30 minutes is a good block, but you could do it hourly (or even every 15 minutes).

Write down everything you've done when the alarm goes off, re-set the alarm and carry on. Here's where you have to be **really** honest though. It's like dieting.

You can cheat and think 'that biscuit didn't count'. Like 'that personal email only took me 30 seconds so I won't bother counting it'.

It counts. Why does a 30 second email count? I'll explain in a bit. *Every action*, from getting up, making a cup of tea, reading that text message or sending a quick Skype, every action should be logged and how long it took.

Let's say we do this over a 5 day period. Monday to Friday, for simplicity, but if you're reading this and it's Tuesday, don't wait until Monday to start. That's the fastest way to not start at all. Start **now**.

By the end of the 5 days, you'll have a big long list of tasks. Many will be the same, I'm sure, both work and non-work related.

Now comes the fun (?!) bit; do this in Excel or on a piece of paper, whichever works out easier for you. (i.e. If you hate using Excel, don't force yourself - just use what come's easiest to you.)

List out your tasks, and count up the time taken for each.

So you'll have things like:

Client Work - 15hrs
Sales Work - 5hrs
...
Facebook - 2hrs

Personal Web Browsing - 2hrs

...

Making Tea - 45mins

Personal Emails - 40mins

You get the idea. There are two things to look at. *How long* you spent doing tasks and *how important* those tasks are.

Using a highlighter, or whatever you have to hand. Mark each entry that matches the criteria "I **must** do this, and it's **important** I do it".

Repeat, with a different mark, for "I **must** do this, at the moment **I'm the only one** who can do it."

Repeat, with "I don't need to do this / this is personal (such as Facebook, Skype, etc)".

I'd then write these out in three separate lists.

The first list, *should* form around 20% of your total time usage. It might not, and don't feel obliged to come telling me the system is flawed if it doesn't - because it doesn't always match exactly, but whatever percentage that first list is, that's what we want to work towards in terms of your working hours on a weekly basis. Let's just say it's 8hrs in a 40hr week. For simplicity.

The second list and third list together should form the other 80%. I would expect, but again it doesn't have to match, that again it would split 80/20. And that the 20% is the third list, the personal time one.

Let's examine the second list first.

This list contains all the tasks that you need to delegate/outsource (I will refer to 'outsource' a lot here, but I mean delegate *or* outsource, it depends on your company structure, the type of tasks, etc).

Many may take the attitude of trying to outsource the biggest tasks first, since they take up most of your time. But that would only lead to defeat, or at least, it'd be a *lot* harder for you to implement.

What you want to do, is start with the smallest tasks first. It kind of reminds me of a story detailed in the book *Switch: How To Change When Change Is Hard* by Chip/Dan Heath, with regards to debt management.

Most accountants/financial advisors will always tell you to start paying off the debt with the biggest interest rate first, because that's the one costing you the most money. Financially it makes sense, but psychologically it's hard.

If you have 10 debts, ranging from £10,000 to £500, paying off the smallest debt first gives you a winning feeling. A sense of accomplishment.

And it's that feeling that is motivational and helps push you forwards to paying off the next smallest debt. And the next. And the next.

The same thing applies with outsourcing your tasks.

I didn't start, for example, by outsourcing the whole development process for our Web Design packages.

I worked with my developer, and showed him the base structure of what we wanted, from the front end. Then I introduced some of the back end. Then I introduced the admin system. As projects flew by, I was doing less and less.

The point of doing it this way is two fold; firstly, it gives you the motivation to outsource more and more, and secondly it gives you a controlled mechanism for doing so. That is to say, you have the ability to maintain the standards you want (this is the biggest roadblock I have had when getting developers to do work for me).

With regards to the personal tasks - be disciplined. Erase them from your daily schedule, turn off Skype and close your email when you're working on set tasks that you *must* do.

I manage this by having a timeline of what I should be doing on a daily basis. I allot times for breaks, which includes opening Skype, having a quick chat with various people and making sure all is OK on the development front.

The reason for this is significant, and this covers why I said earlier thatyou need to include an email that you spend 30 seconds writing in your 80/20 list.

If you're working on a task, for example, you're building a proposal for a client. It's going to take you 30 minutes and you're 20 minutes in, and the phone rings. It might take you just 2 minutes to deal with that phone call, but you can't just carry on with the same flow you had from before the interruption.

It's likely to add another 5 minutes or so before you can get back into the right flow. So a 2 minute call cost you well over 5 minutes.

An email pings in, and you just reply to say "OK no problem" or something. You know, a typical "30 second" response.

The trouble is, the same interruption to your flow means that takes nearly 5 minutes for you to get back into the flow of what you were doing. So a 30 minute proposal actually took 40 minutes. Knowing the frequency of interruptions in the workplace, I know that actually that can end up being more like an hour.

Those distractions, when dealt with separately, might only need to take 10 minutes of your time. If that.

So by being completely 'shut off' from the outside world whilst you're working on tasks, you're more efficient. And efficiency is key. Coming up with this plan is easy. Sticking to it isn't. (But then, I didn't promise everything to grow your Business would be).

It takes practice to be able to ignore the outside world; I know I'm always itching to look at my phone, or to see where that member of staff has just gone, but the more you put that to the back of your mind and focus, the better.

A good technique to create a high performing day is to work in short bursts. If you haven't heard of it before, the pomodoro technique is perfectly suited to this.

Quite simply, plan out the tasks that need to be done. Be ready to work, and clear yourself of *any* distractions. Shut email, close Skype, phone on silent, and any other distractions: ignore them.

Set a timer for 25 minutes and start working. At the end of 25 minutes, take a 5 minute break *but don't open things like Skype.* You'll end up in a conversation which will take far more than 5 minutes. Feel free to check on any absolutely urgent emails that need a one line reply *but don't get involved* - no matter how urgent it can wait an hour or so.

Once your 5 minutes is up, do it again. 25 minutes of solid work, no distractions followed by a 5 minute break. You should do this a total of four times in a row, before then taking a long break. This can be 30 minutes, or in my case, more like an hour or two as I break up my day.

The beauty of this system is, it keeps you highly focused whilst preventing you from becoming fatigued. I know with coding specifically, it can be very draining but the same also applies to tasks such as writing a book (like this one!) and planning out a marketing campaign.

The more you do this, the more you'll become accustomed to it, as will those that work alongside you. They'll learn that they *do not* interrupt your focused time, and in fact, I encourage the use of this technique with my own team - as it brings out the best in everyone.

Expand Your 20% to 40%

So, when it comes to your client base, how do you expand the 20% into 40%?

I'd like to say: easily, because it's not that complicated... but actually, and I'm pretty sure I have written this already, just because it's simple doesn't make it easy. It *is* simple, and you don't need a fancy CRM (Client Relationship Manager) software to do it.

Just a pen, and a piece of paper (if you're OK in Excel I'd recommend that, but this works on paper).

Write down all of your clients you can think of that have bought from you in the last 3 years. If this list is huge because you're E-commerce, you might be better sorting this by a "minimum value" order, so that you don't overwhelm yourself.

For simplicity, let's say we're going to work with 100 names, but it *really* doesn't matter. You could have 10 or

1,000 (although, granted, you'll have your work cut out for you if you have 1,000).

So, once you've got your 100 names, order them by how much they have given you in the last year. Take the top 40, and number them 1-40 - drawing a line through the rest.

From that top 40, then order them by "how easy they are to deal with" - again from 1-40.

Anyone who features in the top 20 both times, put them onto another piece of paper/spreadsheet.

This is your 'top 20%' and your 'ideal customer'. It's pretty obvious, I'm sure, but just to be clear: whilst we want our top client to be a top spender, it doesn't have to be. Because if your top spender is a pain in the arse who ends up eating up huge amounts of your time, or complaining a lot, or just in one way or another uses a huge amount of your time - then they're less valuable than the client underneath them who spends a bit less but is a dream to deal with.

So, now that we have your top 20%, call them. Just phone them for a chat - catch up - find out how they're doing - but most importantly: ask them what you can do for them that you're not doing right now - and **listen**.

What you'll establish out of this, is that there are customers who you want to keep close, and customers you want to keep as far away as possible (although hopefully not from your top 20%).

You can use your top customers list to work out who you want to market yourself to. You can effectively build your own ideal customer (I talk about this later). What would their name be? How old are they? Male/Female? What sort of industry.? So many questions!

Once you've built up your ideal customer (and why not give them a name, something you can relate to) you've got a profile of who you can Market to. I do come back to this in a lot more depth a bit later, because this is actually a really important thing to do.

From the task above (calling your top 20%) you achieve two things. First, you'll bring in more work (I can practically guarantee it). It's always easier selling to existing clients, and it's even easier selling to your *top* clients. Second, you'll also build a profile on your ideal customer, and from your top 20% clients, you'll be able to expand your top 20% to be your top 40%. Then you can start the whole process again, and refine it even more.

Premium Pricing

The main problem with pricing, is that most Business Owners will do 'anything it takes' to get a sale. Often that means dropping the price. But by discounting your price, you're positioning yourself at the lower end of the pricing spectrum, de-valuing your product/service, and you're defining your business as a cheaper business.

When I talk about Premium Pricing, I'm still talking about giving people value for money (i.e. I'm not suggesting you adopt premium pricing for a low value product) - that's not what this is about. In fact I'm always focused on giving people value for money, *but* ensuring you get the maximum price you can, to ensure your business grows and is secure in troubled economic times.

There are a few ways you can approach 'Premium Pricing', but first - the hardest thing to do here is to shift your thinking. Many business owners don't value themselves highly enough, and think that because they don't have the right experience or credibility they can't charge a premium price.

This is nuts, because you can be competing against other people who have a ton of experience, but their service and/or product is awful. If you deliver a good service that's worthy of a premium price - you should be charging that premium price.

Having had this discussion with people before, alongside my own personal experiences - you may find that you need to 'sack' some customers.

Can you really do that?! Sack customers?! Yes. It's one of the most therapeutic things to do if you have a troublesome client, but also a financially rewarding one too if you have a client who's a bit of a drain.

I have done this before, and I should make it clear, unless they're a *real* problem client, I don't mean just turning around and telling the customer to get lost, especially customers who you have been with for a while.

The best way to handle them is to ease them through the process. Perhaps provide plenty of warning that you're changing your Business Model, and that it's unlikely you'll be able to support them in the future in the way that you've been able to in the past.

And remember, going back to what I've talked about sorting your 'top clients' out. Just because they're financially rewarding doesn't make them a 'top client'. But remember how easy they are to work with plays a part too, so just because they don't feature in your top 20% financially rewarding list doesn't mean they're not a 'top client' either.

But if they don't feature in your top 20% of both financially rewarding *and* being a pleasure to deal with, you probably need to ask them to move on. It goes without saying here that you should *always* treat your customers with respect - whether they're giving you £1 or £100,000. But, you shouldn't treat them *equally*.

Treat the top 20% like Gods and give them the ultimate best service (not that the other 80% deserve *poor* service, mind you, but your 20% must get extra benefits).

So who do you select to 'sack'? It's actually pretty obvious... I'm sure you've worked it out, right? Well, simply run the same 80/20 exercise but in reverse. Essentially, find your bottom 20%.

Find that percentage of your customer base that are just nothing but trouble. They expect everything but want to pay nothing. They take up huge portions of your time and the rewards are nothing like they should be.

It reminds me of a client I used to have, who was actually paying us relatively well on the face of it, but when you factored in the amount of work involved from all staff members, it worked out we were earning around £3 an hour from that work. The total amount needed to pay the staff was something like £15 an hour or more (I can't quite remember, it was a long time ago).

If you're worried about confronting the client and asking them to leave, find a local competitor and have a chat with them. Explain you're changing business model and have a few clients that need looking after. Perhaps stroke their ego a bit - "I've heard good things about you..." or something similar.

Then rather than sacking directly, just fire off an intro email or equivalent to both parties and explain again - you're changing business model and can't look after them, but X here is going to take over.

It's then down to the client, sure, but you're easing the transition - they don't have to find another supplier - you've done that bit for them. Easy.

Split testing

A good way to test out various changes in your marketing, is split testing. Split testing allows you to test a lot, from content changes, images, etc, to pricing. But before I dig into exactly what split testing is, how do you measure the success/failure of a marketing piece in the first place?

We use a Conversion Rate. A Conversion Rate is pretty much as it sounds; imagine one hundred people come to your Website, and one person buys something or enquires.

Your Conversion Rate would be 1/100 or 1%. Conversion Rates vary wildly, often based on a multitude of factors, from the "traffic source" to the ease of purchase or enquiry. It can come down to tiny things, such as minor wording changes, a single word can make a massive difference.

So that's why we use Split Testing.

Split Testing is where you run 2 or 3 almost identical pieces of copy and see which works best.

In the world of Pay Per Click, you have two lots of Split Testing.

One, is that you set up two or three pages that are identical except for one small difference. Perhaps a headline or even just a word, sometimes. Then you set up multiple identical ads which link you through to the different versions, and measure which pages are most successful.

The second is that you do this to the Ads. You can run them to the same landing page, but run 2-3 different Ads, i.e. just one word is different.

Often you can do both; then you're optimising the Click Through Rate (CTR) of your Ads (which has another benefit, and we'll focus on a lot more of in the Pay Per Click section), along with the Conversion Rate of the page.

It really is as simple as it sounds. Of course, it applies to pretty much everything.

If you're running an Ad in the paper, you can run one Ad one week, and adjust the Ad for the next. Measure the difference, and enhance the better performing one.

Of course, as I'll come to later, this is one reason why I don't use or rely on SEO (Search Engine Optimisation) for sales. You can't split test a "normal" page on your Website.

Tiered Pricing

This works really well if you've got services you can add to create an additional value. For example, you may start at a 'Bronze' product which covers the absolute basics, and then have a 'Silver' product which is almost like your standard features, and then a 'Gold' product which has a variety of extra 'added value' features.

The benefit of the tiered structure is that as it's more successful you can add additional tiers – for example you could add a Platinum tier later down the line to add in additional features.

Remember though, the really big thing about pricing that I went into earlier:

Your potential customers don't care how long you've been in business, they don't care about how great your product or service is, and they don't care about how much it costs.

You might be convinced that people will always be looking for the best deal or cheapest price. Going back to what I said earlier, a percentage of people will buy solely on price, but those people will often be much harder to deliver for.

Price buyers often seem to want "the moon on a stick".

I'm not saying you shouldn't give great customer service and be attentive to your customer's needs. However if you focus on the bottom end of the market and allow yourself to sell to that price buying percentage specifically - which may be an easier sell initially – you will find your time is completely absorbed by dealing with requests, returns/issues or more.

Positioning yourself at the higher end of the market simply makes your life easier; and in the long run, more rewarding.

Remember if people bought on price, Apple would not be nearly as successful as they are. People wouldn't be driving around in high end cars that cost £50k+ and you wouldn't have people living in huge houses in attractive locations. People buy *based on what they want.*

They buy based on desire – the desire to have your product solve their problem or need.

Remember that your product solves their problem, and make sure you communicate that effectively when you're selling.

CHAPTER THREE

The Three Ms

Market, Message, Medium

To produce anything of substance requires a level of skill, whether it's a web development project such as a complex website, or a physical development project such as a block of flats.

Not only is it dependent on the people developing/creating it, but the success also comes down to a significant amount of planning and hard work.

Even though I don't personally code that much anymore (if at all), I still get involved in the project management, and sometimes I'm really reminded of how terrible other companies are when it comes to development. I see this when I'm looking at what we're taking over or replacing.

An example I encountered a while ago, was a Website designed purely for eCommerce developed on the back of a 'blog' based Website.

This is both pretty uncommon and a bad idea.

It's like trying to put a Ferrari engine in a Ford Fiesta, or like trying to get Vegetarians to go to a Hog Roast.

It won't end well, even if you can get the two together.

But even worse than that is that a lot of the time, that's what most Business Owners are doing with their Marketing.

Because they don't factor in the Three M's.

Market, Message, Medium.

Before you even begin to build your Marketing strategy, you need to know: *Who is your Market?*

How many of them are there? (This is actually very important).

Where are they?

How old are they?

Are they Married? Single? Kids?

How much money do they have?

These questions and so many more form your target profile, and the worst thing you can do is pick your Medium, then find your Message and Market to fit around it.

It'll only end in tears. You *need* to factor in all three for a successful campaign. Take away one, and you can get anything from zero results to poor results.

Focus on the Market or Message first, then find the Medium.

I personally prefer to do it in this order: Market, Message, Medium.

Market

How do you define your Market?

It's actually remarkably easy. I learnt how to do this from Jon McCulloch, a pretty much certified genius in marketing. I have two 'characters' that I may come into contact with in Business.

Andy is the first. I like Andy. Andy is a friendly guy, ranging from his early 30's to late 40's/early 50's. He's probably married, with kids. I don't know his political views but he's almost certainly *not* left wing.

Andy has been running a business for quite a long time, and is trying hard to go from small business to medium business. He's massively frustrated with existing web design/marketing companies who promise the world but never deliver.

He's achieved some good results but never anything 'spectacular'. Having tried things like Google AdWords and never made it work, he holds the opinion it probably doesn't work for him, although he's willing to give it another try it in the right circumstances.

The thing is with Andy, he accepts advice that is given and lets you get on with it. It means he's very easy to work with.

Then there's Chris. Chris, probably a total leftie, has been trying to get his Business off the ground for ages. He's bought loads of books on Business but never really read them all.

He too has used a variety of Web Designers, but always struggles to get anywhere and ends up in an argument because unlike Andy, he's only ever had a maximum budget of a few hundred pounds. He kind of knows a bit about HTML so doesn't see why Web Designers should be paid so much if he can do half the work himself. He ends up micro-managing every project and complaining when it doesn't look or, more importantly, work how he wants.

He has no real focus on his products/service, and what he does sell is mediocre at best. He doesn't want to give any guarantees, even though he's been told he should, because he doesn't want the aggravation of returns.

He's always busy even though he hasn't got much work on, and even though he knows he probably needs to delegate some of his workload, he never will. He's a complete control freak.

When he has got Marketing companies to run his campaign, he's interfered at almost every point (because he has an opinion on everything), and then places the blame on the Marketing company when it doesn't work.

Now if you know me personally, you know that Andy is actually quite like me. And that's no coincidence.

I have built that profile of Andy based on who *I* want to deal with. Not who wants to deal with me.

If I took the last 5 years as a case study, I have worked with more Chris's than Andy's. But now, I'll only ever work with an Andy. If I get a Chris, and I can usually sniff that out quite early, I'll pass him to a competitor or he'll be put off by my marketing funnel.

The thing is, by working with Andy more than Chris, I'll have a happier life, a more productive life, and a more profitable life.

It's obviously no co-incidence that Andy is a lot like me. I have shaped Andy based on my personal views, likes and dislikes. I have shaped Chris in much the same way, just the opposite.

The point is here, by defining these two people, I can relate more easily to whom I'm targeting and I have a clear indication early on as to whether I'm going to want to work with someone. I almost have a checklist of 'acceptable attributes' to work with.

Try it yourself; build your own Andy / Chris, or Jane / Sarah. Build your profile of who you want to work with and who you don't. Then compare that to your Customer base.

Don't treat it like Gospel obviously; there's flexibility. I don't expect every client I deal with to share the exact same political views as me, for example - but I do want them to share more Andy attributes than Chris. Essentially, and this is what it really boils down to, you want your potential clients to be *easy* to work with, rather than a constant stream of aggravation.

Message

So, now that you know *who* you're targeting, you need to work out what you're saying to them.

But here's the real key: by knowing exactly who you're targeting, you can talk to them in the right way. This is how you get your Advert Copy, or whatever it is they're reading, to appeal to them.

Don't get me wrong, you don't have to go as specific as I have, I have simply made choices to *only* deal with those that have the same views as me - because I enjoy dealing with them more - also, because I can.

That's because I chose to, *before* I could afford to choose to. That's a bit of a confusing line, I know, so let me put it this way: If I had waited until I could afford to choose who I was doing business with, I would still be waiting. By sacking the worst Clients and only working with who I wanted to work with, not only was I immediately happier, but everything was more profitable.

Regardless of how similar your character might be to you, you still have to deal with the fact that *they don't know they're similar to you*. In fact, depending on what you do, they're quite possibly even sceptical about dealing with "people in your industry".

I certainly face that problem.

So I get around that with a lengthy lead generation process. My initial advert is traditionally to give something away. Perhaps even this book - either for a low price or free, depending on what I'm testing.

I tend to find that those that invest a little in the first place, even if it's just £5, tend to be more serious about doing business with you later down the line.

Nevertheless you still need to find your message. That initial headline and copy of text that's going to convince them to read that little bit further, and then to engage and give you their details.

Your message is more than 'what you say' though.

The best way to describe this is with Explicit and Implicit.

Your Explicit Message is in the words you write; it's the physical message you're conveying. The Implicit

Message is what's effectively implied by what you're saying. You can adjust your positioning and more just from your Implicit Message.

Explicit Message

So your Explicit Message is what you're writing in your Sales Copy. This might be text in a Newspaper Ad or a line of text in a Google Ad.

This is often the thing that most Business Owners get completely wrong, and why the majority of advertisements don't pay off in the way that so many others do.

They're left scratching their heads when they've developed this fancy looking full page advert in a popular magazine, but it's drawn close to zero results.

This is not just the fault of the business owner. Don't get me wrong, like the law, ignorance is no excuse, and you can't blame other designers entirely - but those that specialise in design, (whether that be design for print, or web design), have a responsibility.

The reason these adverts fail to achieve their maximum potential is because they focus on the wrong things.

The reader doesn't care about you, your brand, your logo, your colour scheme, your ethos, your mission statement, your goals, how long you've been in business, how many staff you have. Let me reinforce the point that sums it up: *they don't care about you.*

They care about *what you can do for them.*

That is to say, whatever your product or service is, it solves a problem. A problem they can't easily solve themselves.

Whether it's from food and clothing to providing a recruitment service, the same rule applies.

You make their life easier or better. One of the two.

So your message needs to make that obvious... blatantly obvious.

Implicit Message

Your Implicit Message is what's implied by what you say. For example by saying:

"We don't work with everyone - and we might not be right for you, or you might not be right for us.",

you're implying that you have a set of standards or requirements to work with someone. In fact this is a phrase I include in my Direct Mail sales letters.

You might be more specific and explicit than that, but you get my point.

The point about this though, is that it seriously affects your positioning.

That is to say, where you position yourself in the Marketplace, whether it's as a low end "we'll take £5 instead of £25" or a high end "we don't engage for less than £5,000".

And you really do want to position yourself at the top; not only is it easier to work with people at this level, but it's far more profitable and enjoyable too.

Of course the service has to reflect the price - I don't mean position yourself at the top if you're selling cheap rubbish. Whether you're selling a unique product/service or a product/service that a million other people sell, you can still *position* yourself at the top with your message.

Medium

So the medium is the physical means in which you deliver your message to your market.

Whether we're talking Google, Facebook, Newspapers/Magazines, Postcards, Letters, Telesales, whatever.

The thing is many business owners I know are always looking for the best medium to use, without concern as to whether their market (who you're talking to) or message (what you're saying) is right.

They'll fit the message to the medium they want to use and hope their market reads it.

For example, by posting to Facebook or Twitter 10 times a day.

Some scenarios like that do work, although relying on "organic" posts on Facebook is much like relying on a bike with zero to no brakes. It's all fine whilst you're going along happily, but if something comes up you're going to crash and there's nothing you can do to control it. You can only really control your advertising with Pay Per Click on Facebook.

That reminds me of a time when I was younger. I grew up in the 80's so actually going by todays standards it's a miracle I'm alive apparently, anyway...

This story begins when I was under 16, I can't quite remember when – I think around I was around 14.

I had arranged to go on a bike ride with a friend, but I had a problem. My bike wasn't fast enough. This was a serious problem for a young teenager.

So, I arranged to cycle to a friends house, borrow his bike, then ride on to meet this other friend. To be fair, his bike was pretty awesome - it was damned fast and finely tuned, but there was one problem.

Actually, one quite, major problem, in the grand scheme of things.

The brakes didn't work.

Well, this led to some amusing collisions whilst out on the ride with my friend, but hey - it was a great laugh. Once the fun was over, I decided to head home. I was cycling down a road called Victoria Avenue in my home town, Southend. This road has a few things down it, including a police station.

If you're cycling along the pavement, you cross two roads. The first was all clear so I kept going at speed.

I thought, I'm not far from my friends house (that I'm returning the bike to) now, so let's make the most of it on this stretch.

It was great, up to the point I saw a police car stopped right where I needed to cross. I had a decision to make. Crash into the police car at full speed, or try and skid the bike over and land on my feet somehow.

I figured, if I turned the front wheel whilst trying to brake as hard as possible with my back, I might just be able to pull this off and look really cool.

Man, I did not look cool.

Full on collision with a lamp post. Over the handlebars, and into the post.

I collapsed on the ground, seriously winded and with serious pain all over including pride. I had no choice but to stand up and cough "yep, no I'm fine thanks" to the lady and her daughter that had come up to check if I was ok.

I got back on the bike and took a very sheepish ride back to my friends house, apologised for scratching the hell out of his bike, and rode mine home.

I was lucky that I had only fractured my fingers, which I didn't find out about until about 4 hours later when my mum got home and saw my fingers had turned a kind of blue-black and rushed me to A&E.

Oops.

But my point here is, that if you're not using the right tools, or the equipment you're using isn't up to standard, you're at risk of looking a bit of a muppet, along with getting seriously winded. Or worse.

And if you're using Facebook to regularly post updates out to, and rely on that as a source of business, then you're effectively riding a bike with no brakes. Because whatever Facebook decide to do to the way your posts are displayed to your fan-base, is their decision, and theirs alone. You cannot control it, nor can you have any impact on it. But it can have a big impact on you.

Consider all the people that complained when Facebook really started tweaking their "algorithm", which works out what content to display to people based on what they (Facebook) thought the reader wanted to see.

All of those people were trying to get 'free customers'.

The opposite is true of course, for those of you that harness the Ads system within Facebook to make sure you're targeting the right Market - and you're always going to be delivering the Message because, well, you're paying for it.

I mention Facebook, because it's a good Medium to use. It's useful for almost every business, from Fish & Chips to Accounting.

And their targeting is outstanding, meaning you can really fine tune your efforts to find your Market.

When it comes to more physical Mediums, such as newspapers or magazines, choosing the right one can be tricky. *You* need to be in control of which Medium you choose, rather than the other way around.

Find your Message, define your Market, then find your Medium to deliver that message to your Market.

It's a simple concept, and I think deep down many business owners *know* that, but they forget or get caught up in special offers for advertising in certain places etc.

CHAPTER FOUR

Direct Response Marketing (DRM)

What Is Direct Response Marketing?

There are two types of marketing, Brand Marketing and Direct Response Marketing.

One of the easiest mistakes to make when starting an advertising campaign is to think it's a good idea to do it for "brand awareness". Think of it this way: a multinational multimillion pound company is quite capable of developing a series of brand awareness adverts which use advanced techniques, such as anchoring.

This is where you're conditioned to feel happy or good every time you see their brand, because you watch their adverts on TV which show happy, fun, families (or something) playing together, or something really funny, which is then reinforced with their logo.

That way, when you're in an aisle in a supermarket, and you're provided with a choice of several brands, the one you go for instinctively is the one that made you feel good when you see it, because your mind associates it with the good feelings from the ad.

They're able to spend £25 Million with a combination of TV Ads, Billboards, Paper Adverts and Mailshots. Now, if you've got a product for consumers, and a spare £25 Million - go for it.

But quite clearly, that sort of approach doesn't work for the average small business.

What's even worse, is that that's what most Small Business Owners do, without even realising it. Partly because they're probably influenced by "what everyone else does" and partly because they're proud of their "brand" and want everyone to see it.

The thing is, it really doesn't work well at all, when it comes to advertising in a newspaper, magazine or online.

The added benefit of doing a carefully implemented direct response advertising campaign is, that if done properly it can work as brand awareness as well.

Direct Response is a *measurable* form of advertising that is proven to be highly effective.

You need a call to action, and it should be a convincing, irresistible offer to the reader, which conveys to them not only why to contact you (or provide you with their contact details) but how.

Brand advertising simply wastes money for the small business owner.

Tracking

If you're not able to track the effectiveness of an advert that's running, change it. You **must** be able to test and measure anything you do (this applies to everything, not just advertising).

You can do this in a variety of ways, from the straight forward (asking how/where they found out about you) to the advanced (automatically tagging a contact in your management software based on which advert they clicked on).

You don't have to be a rocket scientist to start tracking; and it's invaluable in the long term.

Another great example of tracking properly, is to send out a batch of postcards to a certain area with a particular offer.

Whether it be a free guide or discount code – it doesn't matter - you either send them to a tracked page on your website so you can measure the success or you get them to call you.

Which is better?

I can't answer that, you have to test and measure to get the results. Anyone who tells you one is better than the other, is wrong.

They're wrong, not because one is better than the other, but because it *depends*. It depends on your market, it depends on your message and your medium, but more importantly it just plain depends on everything you're doing. The paper you advertised in, the quality of the card you used, the font you used, the size of the headline, the size of the phone number… the list is endless.

Common Mistakes

One common mistake people make is to offer a free newsletter. Don't get me wrong - you'll get *some* signups. But really, who cares about a newsletter? What's in it? Why should they give you their contact details?

Don't expect the reader to have any interest in your company, or to take your word for it that the guide you're providing is great.

You still have to sell something that's "free" because you're asking for personal information, you're asking for their contact details. What's the benefit? What's in it for them?

i.e. Simply saying you're the best in your field or you're a dedicated team is irrelevant. By selling the benefits of what you do, not the service itself, you'll generate more business than ever.

This is critical within all your marketing too, it applies to everything you do.

What can *you* do that really benefits the customer, that they can't get anywhere else?

What's your Unique Selling Point (USP). How can you make a difference to their life?

For example, rather than "Number one store in town for Sofa Covers" – you could say "Make your Sofa look brand new again for a fraction of the cost".

The difference? You're selling the benefit, the product is the way they get the benefit.

The customer gets a brand new sofa look, but they've maybe only spent £300 rather than £3000. That's a pretty attractive offer for anyone.

One of the most important factors to grasp here is, that we're not looking for an immediate sale.

OK, sometimes that might happen, and sometimes we might want that. Depending on what you're selling you might be going for a 'lower value' sale first (more on that in a bit) but my point here is - we're just looking to get their details.

We call this 'Opt In' or 'Permission' Marketing.

That is to say, the people that give you their details (the leads) effectively do so with permission that you can send them additional information and subsequently 'sell to them'.

It's a huge mistake to take these details and do nothing with them, or to treat them completely ineffectively, as you'll be wasting your Marketing budget (do you have a Marketing budget?).

There are a multitude of ways to do this, and I'll cover some of the basics but really, sometimes it comes down to using your imagination a bit, too.

What's Your Budget?

This is a question I used to ask a lot.

I was stupid.

I admit that.

This was stupid for two reasons; I did it for a reason though. I did it because I had been 'trained' to go for the sale as soon as possible. So by finding out what their budget was and by coming in under budget, I could be sure of an easier sale than if I was coming in way over budget.

Sometimes, if the project looked hard (or the client looked hard work), I would massively over quote, intentionally knowing I wouldn't get the work, but if I did, it paid enough to cover the extra costs of either dealing with a hard project or a difficult client.

Anyway the thing is, it was stupid, firstly because it let *them* be in control of *my* pricing.

That's just ridiculous.

Secondly, it's stupid because *no-one* should have a Marketing budget.

Your budget should be carefully calculated *per acquisition*. i.e. What are you prepared to spend to get a customer?

Now the smart amongst you, would instantly say "if I can break even on the initial sale, that's enough".

But you can go further than that.

What you're prepared to spend to get a Customer shouldn't be justified by what they're going to spend with you just once. It should be determined by what they're going to spend with you over time.

That's really, really important.

Even if you say to me "I don't get repeat business, they're one off sales" it's still really, really important.

Why?

Because I have yet to see a business that has no room for repeat business AND no room for referrals.

Those two factors should be a strong consideration in your overall lifetime value of a customer/client.

For me, I do value the referrals, and I get them a lot, but for simplicity I don't incorporate that into my calculation on what I'm prepared to spend to get someone.

Our typical client, might be worth in the region of £10,000 to £30,000 over a 3 year period. And from an 80/20 perspective many of our Clients are far above that upper threshold.

So that means if I spend £1,000 to get a Client, I'm over the moon. I could spend up to £5,000 to get that Client - even at the lower value that's still got room for a return (although you obviously have to take profitability into account).

My point here is, even if you sell £1.99 gadgets, you can work out what that customer is worth to you over three years. Factor in perhaps the odd referral, assuming you implement (which you should) a good referral strategy.

That might then leave you with a budget of £10 to get a Customer.

So whilst you have to watch cashflow, you could be driving your Competitors nuts because you're spending 5x the initial sale to get a Customer on board. But you know it'll pay off because they'll have paid you back within 12 months and in years 2 and 3 you're generating profit from that Customer.

Getting The Opt In

OK...so now we're settled on what we need to spend to get a customer/client, how do we start getting them?

You have a multitude of sources for potential customers, and this is where you must start by focusing on the three M's that we covered - Market, Message, Medium.

When you've found a way to target just your Market, deliver the right Message on the right Medium.

I'll focus on more of this as we get deeper into the book, but a typical example is that you run an Ad on Google which is triggered by a certain keyword/phrase. Perhaps someone is looking for an estate agent.

You run an Ad, along the lines of "Thinking of selling? read this first".

They're then taken to a page which lists the benefits of your free guide on choosing an estate agent, and how to avoid the common pitfalls such as X, Y and Z.

In exchange for this valuable guide, all you want in return is their name and email and the opportunity to send them more information.

Over time, you're able to sell in the form of regular Email marketing. But whether you actually sell in your Emails or just deliver interesting content, the point is you're in their Inbox on a regular basis.

They might not read your emails every day, or even open them, but over time they become accustomed to your name. When they choose to buy whatever product/service it is that you sell, the chances are greatly enhanced that they will choose you, rather than returning to Google.

It's also a good way to weed out those that you don't want to do Business with. The types of people you'll have a personality clash with, for example.

Every now and then I'll get an unsubscribe that makes me chuckle - because they'll leave a complaint on their way out.

But it makes me realise that what I'm doing works; because either this person wouldn't have bought from me or they'd have been a nightmare of a client when they did.

The thing is, you can use this to your advantage, and use it as fuel for one of your other daily emails.

Take this quote from one of my Daily Emails:

...but I do just take a little notice (only a little, mind) when someone 'complains' as they unsubscribe. Mainly because I want to watch my complain rates and ensure I don't get slapped by Infusionsoft.

I had to chuckle when I read this comment.... this was from a lady called Di. She took my book from me at an exhibition a while ago, and I explained I would email out daily. You'd have thought that after the first few emails she'd unsubscribe if it was "unexpected". This was weeks ago now.

Anyway, the comment she left as she marked my emails as "unsolicited SPAM" was: "an opinionated daily rant".

Well, she got one thing right: daily.

The thing is, yes, my Emails are opinionated, they are Emails that relate to my opinion and to my outlook on both Marketing and Life. But this is entirely intentional.

They're also, generally speaking, entertaining, but an important point to raise here is, that whilst I get a lot of opt-ins, opens, clicks and unsubscribes, that's not what Email Marketing is all about.

Nope. It's not about open rates, or click rates, or anything like that. Despite what all the other Marketers will tell you.

It's about *one* thing. How much Business have you had as a result of your email marketing? Sales. Cash in the door.

I don't particularly care if I get 1 unsubscribe or 100 unsubscribes a week because I offend everyone with my opinion. I don't really care if I get 56% open rate and 15% clicks. These can be indicators for sure, but they're nothing to obsess over.

I care about whether I'm getting the sales or not. We'll focus on this more in the Email Marketing section of this book. My point here really is lead generation and regular email marketing (when done right) builds you a list of people you want to do Business with, and repels those that don't, into unsubscribing.

CHAPTER FIVE

Your Website

I've got my Website, that's all I need to do… Right?

Having spoken to hundreds of customers and business owners over the last 10 years, one of the most startling revelations is that they spent a sum of money, whether it be £500, £1000, £2000, £5000 or more, on developing a website. Then, they have left it exactly as it is for years - literally years.

This might not be a problem if you had a website developed by a complete Internet Marketing genius who had the foresight to implement all the latest marketing techniques. It might not be a huge problem if the website is generating you more business than you can handle – but that's pretty unlikely (if it was, you probably wouldn't be reading this).

The problem is, one of the most fundamental keys to a successful marketing campaign, whether it be Online or Offline, is "Test & Measure".

There's no point implementing something and hoping it will bring you some business, but then even if it did, you wouldn't know about it because you're weren't measuring the results.

Your website is one of your most important tools, it's where you're going to be directing a huge proportion of your potential clients – either to sign up for something or to buy something (if you're smart, it'll be the former).
So what are the key points for making a successful website?

This varies depending on whether you're using your website as a selling platform (i.e. e-commerce) or whether you're using it to generate leads.

When it comes to developing your website, there are some common points you should adhere to, although it's not *critical* you adhere to these on your main website, these particularly apply on landing pages (I'll come back to landing pages fully in the Pay Per Click section),

• Keep to black on white, at least for the main copy - it's what people are conditioned to read, and they just find it easier. This is more applicable to landing pages than your overall website copy, but a good rule to adhere to.

• Keep line lengths to under 60 characters if you can, this means use columns if you don't already.

• Be wary of over using the colour red, it draws the attention and signifies danger - and this might not be the right thing to do. It can be in some scenarios, but keep it very limited.

• Be completely and utterly focused on "above the fold", i.e. on a standard sized screen, what you can see before you have to scroll down. You have less than 8 seconds to capture the readers attention.

• Make use of a headline, the first 10-20 words should be in a nice big font that gives the customer the reason they want to stay on that website for another 10 seconds.

• Make sure there's a call to action (i.e. a button or similar) visible above the fold. Especially when looking at it from a mobile perspective - make sure the user doesn't have to look far for a call to action when scrolling.

• If you can (and we'll cover this more later) – use a video.

On the note of the Call To Action, in the past we used to say use a form, but interestingly tests have shown that using a button *tends* to give lower bounce rates (a 'bounce' is where someone comes to the page, then leaves straight away - you want this, obviously, as low as possible).

The thought is that this is because the contact form immediately makes the reader realise they have no choice but to fill out a form, so they're not reading the copy. But, by having a button you remove that immediate observation and they're more likely to read the copy, so by the time they're at the button for the call to action they're already "sold".

I'd say in true 80/20 fashion, 80% of our landing pages have the form after a button, so as with everything, it comes down to test and measure. Which performs best for you?

What Type Of Website Do You Want/Have/Need?

There are a couple of types of Website.

One is used solely for selling products; it has, generally, little content other than the products and everything is gearing you towards putting that product in the shopping cart and entering in your credit card details.

The other, is more for lead generation or information. Many refer to these sites as a 'Brochure' site but clearly that's the wrong attitude to take. You want your site to be *more* than a Brochure, you want it to generate you leads/business.

Lead Generator

Lead generator sites do what the name says; they generate leads. Their sole purpose is to act as a brochure / point of contact, and to sell the need for that person to get in touch with you.

If you follow the "common points" I referred to earlier, then you're generally on to a winning site. Although it's worth saying that I don't tend to focus on the 'actual website' for the large proportion of the marketing relating to your website.

"Eh?" I hear you say.

I'm referring to Landing Pages.

These are pages on your website which can *and normally should* link back to your main website, but that can't be reached from the website itself. This is outlined in much more depth in the Pay Per Click section, but in a nutshell, this enables you to test multiple versions of the same page to see which performs best. Along with keeping the distractions to an absolute minimum (such as navigation bars, links / social media links, etc).

The critical thing with the page layout though, is to have a really good headline, and don't make it "welcome to the best XYZ in the country" – everyone says they're the best.

It's annoying and it's meaningless.

Go more along the lines of "We can solve your problem of XYZ by ABC in 3 days".

Something, regardless, that attacks or provides a solution to their problem that led them to be on that page in the first place.

If you're not sure where to begin on this, start listing down what you sell, whether it be product or service.

Next to it, write down why someone would want it - what is its purpose? What problem does it solve? Does it make their life easier? Does it make them more comfortable? Is it just for luxury? Is it an essential? Could they be taking a risk by not having your product?

Find the USP of the product, and find the question that results in your product as the answer.

Then make that your headline.

A good call to action is the next most important thing. There's no point in driving someone to your site, writing a huge amount of fantastic engaging copy, completely hooking them for 5 minutes, and then having no way for them to just say "Yes! Send me more details".

It's insanity.

You would be amazed at how many sites do it. Take a look at yours - does yours do it? If you do have this problem, don't feel bad about – feel great, this means you've got something to improve!

E-Commerce

Let me say this first of all: it is <u>extremely difficult</u> to run a *successful* online-only shop. Rewind 10-15 years and we're talking a different scenario, but unfortunately for you, we're not. If you're running an e-commerce website, then you've *got* to be different.

Let me put it this way - if all you sell are physical products, which are equally available everywhere and anywhere for a variety of prices, you have to do a few things to really make yourself stand out from the crowd.

In fact, it's one of the biggest challenges we have as a marketing company - to get Pay Per Click efficient for online shops.

But I tell you - the key is *not* in getting the first sale. The key is getting the *repeat* sale. How you engineer that is the fun. I would focus on regular Email Marketing for the repeat sales, for sure.

Anyway to run a successful online shop, you've got to make sure your website has several things.

Firstly you should be doing everything a lead-generator site does, in terms of having a good headline and call to action, but you need to make sure your images are big and decent quality. If they're anything but "high resolution" – re-take them.

There's no excuse these days, decent digital cameras are cheap and most smartphones are perfectly fine. They don't have to be professional shots – just decent, although, the more professional the better - a white background pays dividends, but as I say, an iPhone camera is more than good enough.

If you sell items you stock, and the items aren't too big, you can get a cheap lightbox online (search Google/Amazon, you'll find plenty). You put your product in the lightbox, take a photo using your camera on a tripod, and suddenly your photos are amazing.

Secondly, you need to make sure the site is useable. Look at how Amazon works. It doesn't have to be hugely overcomplicated with a ton of features, you've just got to make sure the user can find the product (and the information) they want fast.

I've mentioned landing pages briefly - which I'll come back to - but basically for an online shop these are pages which display only the products the customer has searched for.

Most people I've come into contact with over the years are relatively computer literate, they spend a lot of time surfing the web, so they're able to work out the sites that are maybe a little less intuitive. Many of these people I have come into contact with though, have someone they know that's maybe less technical.

You **need** to find the least technical person you can and get them to buy something.

Think of a random product, and ask them to find it, and buy it.

Give them a card, you can just refund it after.

Watch them from a distance (or if you can't be there, get them to write as much down as possible, but it'll really help if you can be there).

I *guarantee* you'll find yourself wanting to jump in and point things out, say "oh just do this…".

Don't do it.

Observe, make notes, and then change the layout.

If your web designer says "oh you don't want to do that" or "well, I can do it, but it'll take ages to implement" – consider finding another web designer.

You will genuinely be amazed at how much that motivates them to implement what you want.

Take this from me – as a person who has worked in the web design field for over 10 years – most web designers know absolutely nothing about marketing and they're not willing to learn because it impacts on their lovely fluffy designs.

I showed some of the landing pages we implemented to a Web Designer I used to work closely with. He was stunned we released it to a Client, but the thing is, it performed *outstandingly*.

It's not about how it looks, it's about how it reads.

CHAPTER SIX

Pay Per Click

Now for the fun stuff, Pay Per Click...

Can Pay Per Click really be fun? Of course... my point though, is that this is where we really start to knuckle down and get to the good stuff.

Because of the sheer quantity of information about Pay Per Click - this is a bit of a beefy chapter. So I'm going to break up Google/Facebook and LinkedIn into different sections.

Before I get anywhere *near* that, you might well be of the opinion, that Pay Per Click (PPC) is for suckers and you can do it short term whilst you build your Search Engine Optimisation (SEO).

Don't worry - I'll forgive you, this once! (But *only* once...)

Seriously though, there are a bucket of reasons not to focus on SEO, especially as a primary source of traffic. It is not something you actively should spend money on, and you (and I cannot stress this enough), absolutely must not depend on it.

If you are running a business dependent on SEO traffic, you are in a very, very dangerous place. If you're not sure what I'm talking about here, let's just quickly take a moment to explain both.

There are two types of traffic, traffic being 'people visiting your website'. (I always hate the term 'traffic' in the same way I hate the term 'human resources' - sounds far too clinical and corporate for my liking).

There's SEO or 'Organic' traffic, which is where you appear in the main listings of Google, in a position that Google decides based on how important they think the content of your site is.

Then you have PPC traffic, which is where you appear *above* the SEO/Organic listings for a selection of keywords that *you choose* to be shown for; and you choose how often and where to be displayed by the amount you're paying.

Whilst SEO/Organic traffic sounds like the dream, (because if you get to the first page of Google for certain keywords and stay there, you can generate a load of business) paying to get you there is expensive and you have no guarantee you'll stay there in the long run. You simply can't depend on it.

Pay Per Click is the only *guaranteed* way to bring a measured amount of traffic to your site, that you can measure the cost of and gauge results accurately.

It is also the only way you can scale the traffic (i.e. quickly and easily increase the amount of visitors) – you can't really scale SEO.

You can be paying an SEO company anything from £100's to £10,000's per month to do huge amounts of optimisation for you, but there's no way that value can compare to Pay Per Click and there's no way you're *guaranteed* that traffic.

The first rule of Pay Per Click...

Tempting as it is to write "The first rule of Pay Per Click is don't talk about Pay Per Click", it's not that... I'll come to the first rule in just a second. First, I want to explain why there are a couple of reasons that so many business owners *love* Pay Per Click and why SEO as a business model, well, sucks.

First and foremost, Pay Per Click is a way to literally control the flow of leads like a tap, turning it up and down with the budget.

Second, is because of what you can do with Landing Pages. I'll be going into landing pages in far more detail in the next section but for the purpose of my point here - all you need to know is the landing page is where someone lands when they click on your Ad.

You see, one of the *great things* about landing pages, is that you can run identical versions with just one word difference. This is called split testing and it allows you to see which version does better - something you *can't* do with SEO, and that's one key reason why SEO sucks.

So I promised you the first rule of Pay Per Click? Well, it's this...

The first rule of Pay Per Click is that you absolutely **must not,** *under pretty much any circumstances, ever send people to your homepage.*

The *only* exception here, is if your homepage is geared up to be your landing page, which 99 times out of 100 it isn't, and you wouldn't want it to be. Your homepage should be designed to let people navigate throughout all your different products/services. The exact opposite of what you want for a landing page.

When running any form of Pay Per Click or in fact, any Direct Response Marketing campaign, you should **always** send people to a dedicated Landing Page.

So what's a Landing Page?

Let's start off by saying, you can have a variety of types of landing pages. A Landing Page is the page where your visitor 'lands' (i.e. views) when they click an Ad. Or perhaps they get to the page via typing in a web address you've setup such as 'thisismylandingpage.com'.

Why would you set up a domain like that? Good reason which I'll come back to more when talking about advertising offline, but think 'print advertising' (as I'll come to in literally just a second)

Essentially the Landing Page is the page they view when they respond to your Ad. Whether that's clicking an Ad on Facebook, clicking an Ad on Google, or typing in an address found on a print advert. (This is where you realise that mycompanyname.com/product is boring but fixmybrokenthing.com is far more interesting and more memorable).

There are a good few companies out there for Landing Pages. I now exclusively use OptimizePress, and I'll detail why shortly. That's not to say *you* should - in fact there are loads of great suppliers, including LeadPages and Instapage amongst others.

LeadPages has these things called 'LeadBoxes' which are hugely awesome and effectively let you embed opt-in email forms pretty much anywhere - perfect if you're not a developer and want to do this yourself.

Why do I use OptimizePress? Simple, really. It integrates with the platform we use (WordPress). But it's the most flexible from my point of view, i.e. It fits my need. I'm a developer at heart, so it's no problem for me to do the odd CSS tweak here or there.

If you have no idea what CSS is, you probably want to stick to LeadPages or similar. We needed to choose one platform for consistency, and OptimizePress was it. That might change in the next year - who knows? But at time of writing, that's what we're using.

So, in summary, a landing page is where people 'land' when clicking through from an Ad. Simple, really, eh?

I also mentioned squeeze pages. A Squeeze Page is a *type* of Landing Page. It can have 10 words on it or 10,000 - but the point is it goes nowhere and only has a form on it for the reader to fill out.

i.e. Fill out this form and give us your details, or go away.

Squeeze Pages work well when they're put in to place in the right way, but they're not always the right solution for every campaign.

So what other landing pages are there?

Well, pretty much anything you need really - Squeeze Pages are most often used because people are so very easily distracted.

You can use landing pages as a way to sell individual products, or as a launching page to go to a range of products.

You can use landing pages as a way to introduce a service, or even launch a 'product & service'.

What I mean by that leads to a story about a time I tried to study myself. It's quite a hard thing to do, because you know you're being studied, by yourself, so it's really hard to be objective.

We're all used to seeing Ads on Facebook; it's one of the things they've managed to implement *really* well now. It's part of your news feed, and most people don't even realise it.

Well, ok, they *know* they're Ads, but a lot of the time they don't realise they're being sold to until they're sold on the product and are reaching for their credit card.

Some time ago, though, I saw an Ad for some dog food.

I'm always running out of dog food - it's a real problem for me.

So the headline "Never run out of dog food again" was particularly catching.

I clicked through and this very nicely implemented landing page explained to me how, if I pay just £x (I think it was something like £20) a month, I can have dog food delivered to me regularly. They calculate how much

I feed the dog based on his age/weight/etc, and subsequently know when to send the next batch of food.

And the winning deal - the first 6 weeks of food was just £1.

Not only did this seem like a steal, but I had buckets of respect for the company for doing it. They were proving that what they had was awesome, and they *knew* that the *majority* of the Customers who bought it for £1 would continue their subscription.

Yes, you'll have some who will simply cancel immediately, taking the £1 worth of food, abusing the system, but you'll always get that.

However if you got 100 Customers, and even 80 of them cancelled, as long as that 20 that remained were profitable enough to pay for sending out that first batch (say, within the first year?) then you'd do that all day long.

The second instance was for Coffee. I saw a headline ,"The Smell Alone Is Ridiculous", with a picture of some Coffee. Being a Coffee drinker, it naturally grabbed my attention (as intended, I'm sure).

I went through to another landing page, which carefully guided me through how to get my first batch of coffee for, you guessed it, £1.

As soon as I saw that, I thought: I *had* to trial the experience.

So I went through and purchased some coffee. What I *really* liked about this, was that they almost forced you to choose - do you want Coffee every 1 week or 2 weeks?

This meant that the people that completed the transaction had agreed to get coffee on a regular basis.

Now I liked this, but it was too frequent for me. A mistake on their part I feel, but nevertheless an amazing system, and I guarantee you that with the level of commitment they made they'll have done very well out of that campaign.

The third experience, and I was almost looking out for these sorts of Ads now, was for shaving.

I don't quite recall the exact headline, but I think it was along the lines of "Do you shave? Never run out of toiletries again". It could have been better, being that they pretty much only supplied razors (well, and the shaving gel etc, but it's the razors that would catch most peoples eye).

Anyway, they had this particularly swish looking razor with some initials engraved on it. Who wouldn't want their initials engraved on their razor?!

Going through the order process, I was able to get £10 off my first delivery of both the razor handle and enough blades to last 6 weeks. I think it cost £10 for me to get started, but again based on "how often do you shave" they then knew when to send me the next batch.

And of course, in all three of these scenarios, payment was *extremely easy* and I had to do nothing special to get the recurring payments working - meaning unless I actually went in and cancelled, they'd just assume I want more stuff and they would charge me more money.

Google Search

If you've not got involved in Pay Per Click and especially Google AdWords before, the best thing to do is sign up for an account. You need to experience the interface, even if you don't actually end up running it yourself, you need to see it.

Your choice of platform really, is Google or Bing. I would, if you're just starting out, focus on Google initially. Bing is great, and the system is almost identical to Google, but I would only move to Bing once you're running at "max budget" on Google. That is to say, when you're bidding for all the keywords you want with a virtually unlimited daily budget.

So for now go to www.google.co.uk/adwords (or if you're not in the UK, google.com/adwords), or just search Google for adwords, but be wary of agencies running their own Ads for people looking for AdWords - no reason you can't use them in the future but my point here is, you need to see it direct first.

Once you've signed up you'll need to create a campaign.

As you're creating this, Google automatically selects "Search Network with Display Select". i.e. the ads you create will display for both people searching for things, and people who are just browsing the web.

The way Google have changed this over the last year or so (at time of writing, which is 2016) has made it better than it used to be but, I think, is still the completely wrong approach to running a campaign.

You absolutely *must* run them separately and I recommend you select "Search Only (All Features)".

Why is this so important?

Search & Display networks are totally different things, and you need your campaigns, ad groups and landing pages to be as specific as possible.

Both Search & Display have a very different Click Through Rate (CTR), which is shown as a percentage and reflects the number of clicks your Ad has got compared to how many times it's been displayed. i.e. if it's been shown 100 times and got 1 click, it's 1%.

Something worth saying here is, CTR is really important, but not the *overall* factor that it used to be when measuring your Quality Score.

Google, much like they do with their Search Engine Optimisation, are constantly improving how the Pay Per Click engine works.

It used to be that your position was as simple as whoever bid the most.

But then that means you have people with more money, who are able to outbid others, get a higher position though not necessarily the best content.

Over time they introduced a variety of factors that also impacted your position.

Now CTR is just one of the factors that determines your Quality Score, which is subsequently partially used to determine your Ad Rank, which determines where the Ad is placed.

The higher the Ad Rank – the higher the position on the paid for ads.

So what can you do to get a better quality score? What else impacts your position?

Well, it's important to know this book isn't a guide to Google. Things, including the layout of Google

AdWords, change quite quickly, (relatively speaking, in terms of writing a book) so I'm not going to focus on specifics.

The Aim Is To Break Even...

First and foremost though, one of the keys to success you'll have with Google (and in fact any Pay Per Click), is to lose the strong focus on Cost Per Click (CPC).

The CPC is normally what most people focus on, and it's the biggest roadblock to people not taking up Google AdWords in the first place. And this is, unfortunately, seriously misguided.

OK, that might be a little harsh, but too many times I've dealt with say, a plumber, who won't pay £5 per click to run Ads for people looking for a boiler install. It doesn't matter what it is per click, because it depends on what it is per lead. This is referred to as Cost Per Action or Cost Per Acquisition (CPA).

And it's CPA that we really focus on.

Because it's CPA that determines whether you're going to be profitable or not.

Let's take the boiler example.

Overall cost of job: £3000
Cost of boiler/parts: £2000
Cost of labour: £500
Profit: £500

If it took 200 clicks to get 5 leads, and one of those to go ahead, you'd be down by £500.

If it took 100 clicks to get 5 leads, and one of those to go ahead, you'd be breaking even.

If it took 50 clicks to get 5 leads, and one of those to go ahead, you'd be £250 ahead.

These figures are pretty crude, but they represent the overall approach we need to take with PPC. That the CPA should be less than or equal to the profit of the job.

"Surely it should be less than the profit of the job" I hear you shout.

We're just talking about simply acquiring customers here. With Pay Per Click the most successful businesses are those that engineer repeat business over and over.

"My product purchase is always a one off" I hear you cry again.

Even if your product is a one off purchase, there are ways to engineer repeat business. And on top of that there are ways to engineer referrals.

So how do we focus on making sure the CPA is right?

Refining The Process

Remember, and burn the phrase into your head, "It's a marathon, not a sprint".

The success to Google AdWords is constant refinement. It needs constant attention, and it's about making use of all the features available to you.

Remember that the more you keep Google happy, the more traffic you'll get for your money. The way you do that? Simple.

Keep your landing pages relevant to your ads, which should be relevant to your keywords in small, defined sets of ad groups. Don't worry if you have no idea what I mean here - you can find out more in some free resources I'll tell you about at the end of the book.

Geo-targeting

Targeting by Geographic location may be relevant because you're a bricks and mortar business looking for local people, or it can be used where your budget might be a bit limited.

Let's say you have a limited budget and you're targeting people who are looking to sell their property anywhere in the UK. Your budget will be used up *much* quicker if it's a campaign targeting the whole of the UK, rather than say, Essex.

This is pretty straight forward, and comes down to the number of people searching in Essex which is going to be far less than the whole of the UK. So by targeting only people in Essex we significantly reduce the number of people who may see and click on the Ad.

Even if you are a national company, it can still be worth running local campaigns. The reason for doing so is, it allows you to more easily track statistics and trends of conversion rates, as you might find that people in the South East convert to more paying Clients than people in the North West. This can be very useful if you're spending significant amounts of money in generating your leads.

Keep It Simple, Stupid

Don't make it complicated by trying to keep it simple. What I mean by this is, you *need* to start out with a structure.

Don't just throw a load of keywords into action and wait to see what performs. I mean, sure that's better than doing *nothing* but it's not as productive as it could be.

The general structure with Google AdWords is that you have a Campaign. And in a Campaign, you have Ad Groups. In Ad Groups you have ads and keywords. When people search for something, they're shown an ad from the ad group which your keyword matched.

In an ideal world you want no more than a few keywords in an Ad Group, which should have two almost identical ads (for split testing).

Obviously, the ad text should be tied very closely to the specific keywords (i.e. the keywords in the group should also be related to each other very closely).

This way, the ads that you run on that group will be far more relevant to your keywords, and the ads that are served in relation to your keywords will be more relevant, which results in a higher click through rate and your quality score will be higher.

This might all sound really complicated, but it really is simple.

This way, when you're looking at your campaign, you'll have a list of Ad Groups that detail the small set of keywords in each one.

It means you can look at an Ad Group, and see the overall performance of the very similar keywords. If you have just one or two Ad Groups with hundreds of keywords, not only is it harder to work out which keywords perform the best, but your Quality Scores for all your keywords will be impacted by the worst performing keywords.

That is to say, if you have 100 keywords and 10 perform great but 90 perform terribly, your 10 great ones will be dragged down by the 90 terrible ones.

Don't be a cheapskate

You *have* to be prepared to spend more initially, not for long, but you need the CTR as high as possible.

If you bid higher in the early stages of the campaign, you force your ads to a higher position whilst the click through rate is low (although, this won't last for too long as your number one position is driven by such a wide variety of factors), which means they get more visibility and more chance of building a good quality CTR faster. Remember, by making your Ad Text relevant and catchy and keeping the ads grouped to just a few keywords, your Ad Text is more likely to engage the user and get them to click (thus getting a higher CTR).

You could bid £20 per click, but if your Ad text means people don't want to click, your CTR will fall. And no matter how high your bid, you won't remain at number one.

It's not just about the Ad Text

Quality Score is determined by Ad Relevance, the Click Through Rate and the Landing Page Experience and what Ad Extensions you use.

So whilst the Ad text is important, and you need to use as many Ad Extensions as possible, (I'll come back to this) it's critical to make sure that the relevance of their search query is carried on to the page which they "land" on when they click your link (the "landing page").

There's absolutely no point showing the customer your homepage when they've searched for "ceramic teapots".

Take them to a page full of ceramic teapots!

Your conversion ratio is guaranteed to be higher, but also Google will pick up on the fact that the landing page is more relevant, and subsequently your quality score will be higher.

Focusing on Google Search is great, but...

You're missing out on an absolutely huge opportunity if you don't focus on a well delivered Display Advertising campaign.

Why?

Well, look at it this way: how much of your day do you actually spend searching? Most of your average day will be taken up with your day to day activities or casual surfing.

What does this mean?

It means that for the vast majority of the time, every single customer you could ever want is targetable using one of these three display advertising platforms.

You might say "Banner adverts? Oh I don't click on those..."

Well, OK. You might not click on those for 99.99% of your browsing usage, but if you looked at your history over the last year, is it possible that in that 0.01% of time you might have clicked on a banner/display advertisement that caught your interest?

I didn't pick 0.01% at random – it's a common CTR (Click Through Rate) for display advertising. Between 0.01% and 0.03%.

Why bother with such a tiny percentage?

Because of the amount of impressions (people who have the opportunity to see your ad).

Think about it. If 1,000,000 people could view your ad over the course of 1 week, with a CTR of 0.01% you could have 10,000 clicks.

The CPC (Cost Per Click) tends to be lower, so you're not paying the same as someone searching for something, but that's equally reflected in the number of conversions – it will tend to be much lower with display advertising. Once you're doing everything in this book, you'll find that your conversions increase anyway, so you really can't lose.

So now we've established that Display Advertising is worth doing, how can we do it and how can we get the most out of it?

Targeting.

With all the display platforms, you get the incredible ability to pick and choose who you're adverts are going to be displayed to.

Imagine that, 15 years ago, someone said, "Yes, you can have an advert in my paper. It's read by 100,000 people but I can guarantee you that only men, aged 30-40 who live in this certain postcode and who happen to like golf, will read it".

It would have seemed like an impossible dream, but between Facebook, LinkedIn and Google Display Advertising, you have all of those options and more.

Google Display: Traditional Profiling

The traditional profiling route means you can select potential viewers of a certain age, by their interests, by what sort of site the banner will display on, and a whole host of other options.

I recommend you take a look at the options in as much detail as possible, and consider your target market. It will be critical to making this a success.

You want the sites the ads are displayed on to be relevant, you want the viewers interests to be in the right field for what you're selling / promoting (ignore re-marketing for the minute, we'll cover that shortly) and as usual you can specify by gender or age.

Remember, these are approximations, it's not the accuracy Facebook or LinkedIn will give you, as the majority of Facebook/LinkedIn targeting is built up on their actual profile – but it's still pretty accurate.

Re-Marketing

Re-marketing is huge. We've all seen it, right? You've been looking at a new set of pots & pans on Amazon, and then an hour later the same pots & pans are advertised to you on Facebook.

It's amazingly powerful. It works whereby the user visits your web page, a cookie is placed on their PC, and then as they browse around other sites your advert can be displayed, because you know they've seen your site.

There are re-marketing options for Google and Facebook, I'll come back to Facebook, but for Google it's really easy to set up.

Again, because things change, I don't want to do a step by step (Google Support will help you with that) - but in a nutshell, when logged into AdWords in your Campaigns you should find something called Shared Library.

Click in to 'Audiences' and click 'New' then 'Remarketing list'. The settings after that are relatively straight forward, a name of the list, membership duration (can be up to 540 days!) and a description.

You also have 'Who to add to your list'. You can select "Visitors of a page" or "Visitors of a page with a specific tag".

The 'tag' allows you to track certain conversions (or lack of – which can be very useful for tracking abandoned carts, for example, if they got all the way to the credit card bit, then stopped).

So if you're *really clever* (and we do this) you can take people back to the exact same point they were at, and simply get them to complete the sale.

The tag is simply a bit of JavaScript code – if you don't manage your website just send it to your web designer and they can put it in for you.

Facebook Pay Per Click

Many Marketers will tell you, Social Media is the way forwards. They're not wrong about that, but they are wrong when they say you need to build your likes and shares, and get lots of 'engagement'.

The real success for Facebook, comes in the form of the examples I gave earlier, where you're getting people *off* Facebook on to your own website, and getting their details or getting them to purchase something.

Or even better, selling them into a Subscription.

If you haven't got a Facebook account – get one. You don't have to put your real name or profile picture up there if you're worried, no-one will ever see it.

This is often the biggest objection I face when I tell people about it.

They "don't want to be found".

Fair enough, but if you want your business to be found, get to grips with it, because it'll pay you dividends in the long run. And the main thing is, there are lots of people with the same name, so - if you don't want to be found, don't upload a profile picture and ignore any Friend requests; simple.

Chapter 6: Pay Per Click

You need to get a Facebook Page; don't worry so much about the Likes, we're not worried about how many likes your page has. We're using it as a base for your Ads, and in the long term, you'll build likes anyway as a side effect of the Ads.

But we really don't care about Likes.

Again, because things change so rapidly, I'm not going to go into *huge* detail here, and certainly no step by step - because the basics don't tend to change and that's what's most important here.

With the Facebook ads, you get very fine control over the targeting. The main targeting options are:

• Location: you can specify a country, region or town and specify how many miles radius. This lets you make sure you can run your ads just to people in your area if you want.

• Age & Gender: as it sounds, you can specify the lower and upper age limit of the viewers of the advert, and whether it's men, women or both that view.

• Interests: this one is really interesting, this allows you to target on the fact that they like Golf, but they may not have actually specified that anywhere in Facebook – it's done purely on the pages they "Like" and the activities they do.

• "Interested In", "Relationship status" and more: There are many other filtering options which are always changing and improving. Make sure you take the time to

87

read the rest of the options and target it any way possible.

In a nutshell, you can advertise very specifically with Facebook. And we know that by determining our market, like my Andy and Chris figures, we can almost certainly find the right market to deliver our message to.

Most people when they set up an Advert Campaign, want to get it seen by as many people as possible.

I try to get it seen by as few people as possible, because the more specific your Ad is, the more profitable it will be. I would rather have 10 specifically targeted eyes looking at my ad than 10,000 untargeted.

Also, as a result, the higher the likelihood that you'll get it seen by an Andy, not a Chris.

LinkedIn Pay Per Click

There are scenarios where Business to Consumer, might work, and it entirely depends on what you're selling… but primarily? I'd focus on Business to Business with LinkedIn.

Remember, the secret is to get them *off* the Social Media, whatever that may be, and on to your own site.

Obviously it depends on the Business but many people are far more likely to get away with visiting LinkedIn than Facebook during the day.

In some jobs it's a requirement. But that aside, what's really interesting is the advertising opportunities.

In a similar way to Facebook, you can really drill down on the targeting with LinkedIn, but it has a couple of really special features that you don't get with Facebook.

You're able to display adverts to people in a particular industry, with a particular job title or job function/seniority, by their skills, and even by what School they went to.

Advertising on LinkedIn is a little harder than Facebook, in that getting the click-throughs can be a lot harder.

And they're more expensive than Facebook, but generally the quality is better too. That is to say, if someone clicks they're more likely to engage.

Remember to make sure you're sending the user to a highly specific landing page.

In my case, I tend to ensure the Google, Facebook and LinkedIn pages all are tracked separately. That is to say, if someone fills out a form on a LinkedIn landing page, when they enter the CRM (I use InfusionSoft) it 'tags' the contact with the appropriate source.

That way I can look at InfusionSoft, and see that this week 25 contacts have come from LinkedIn, 45 from Facebook and 100 from Google.

CHAPTER SEVEN
Email Marketing

The Myth: People Don't Want Your Email

Yeah, so here's another common myth for you: People don't like receiving emails from you.

It's completely wrong.

What people *don't* like is irrelevant sales letters, newsletters or unsolicited email (SPAM).

Can you really make use of email (and send emails every single day) to build a long term relationship with a potential customer, who then might convert later down the line? The answer is simple: Yes you can.

And before you start with the "That's fine, but it wouldn't work for my business" attitude, this works for *every* business.

So where do we start?

Firstly, you should do a little segmentation. You don't always need to, for example, my daily emails (yes, that's right, daily) go out to both new and existing clients. But you should be able to email just your existing customers, and just your new potential customers, or people that have expressed an interest in a particular product or service.

Incidentally, if you're segmenting contacts on an automated basis - remember to move customers from the potential list to existing list once they've converted!

The easiest way to build a long term relationship is to tackle some problems in your industry.

"52 things to avoid when hiring someone".

On the landing page (the "opt in" page, where they give you permission to email them) you give them 3 things to avoid and then "enter your first name and email here to get the rest". You can then have 49 further emails scheduled to send to them.

For this to work successfully, you absolutely *must* have an auto-responder. An auto-responder is something that allows you to pre-set emails and send after a set period of time – i.e. "1 week after joining the list", "2 weeks after joining the list", etc.

There are many auto-responder solutions out there, and for the non-technical there are some easy solutions. I have used a huge variety over the years, many for myself, for testing, and many for clients.

If you're really new and just starting out, Mailchimp is a good place. I really, *really* like InfusionSoft, but also Ontraport is good.

Incidentally, I first realised this theory that "you *need* email marketing software" about two years prior to writing this book originally. A year later, as I go over it again, I realise how *fundamental* it is. I genuinely can't see any reason why if you were looking to do *any* sort of email marketing software, you wouldn't set yourself up with the basic Mailchimp or equivalant account.

Personally, and this is *personally*, I couldn't function without Infusionsoft. So much so that I'm planning to develop our own system, though this could take years to come to fruition - primarily because of the level of complexity but also because, quite simply, Infusionsoft works *really* well. It has pretty much all the right functionality in all the right places.

Positioning

Depending on where the person has come from, you may or may not want to jump straight into 'sales' emails.

I tend to avoid sales emails initially, as I focus on people looking for information, i.e. they're not in a position or prepared to buy.

Your email marketing should either be providing useful, helpful information that develops the fact that you're an authority on your subject, or provide entertainment.

It's often best, I believe, to do the former first, and the latter second.

That is to say, you have an indoctrination period, whereby you set your positioning up (i.e. you're an authority on the subject) and provide useful information.

Once they move off the Auto Responder, they then settle on your broadcast list.

Your broadcast list should be the place where they then "raise their hand" to indicate interest in a product/service, which then subsequently results in additional or separate emails on the subject. More on that in a bit though.

Keep It Interesting

It's important to remember to keep your emails interesting. People engage with a story. Here's a good example - think about your time in School or College.

How engaged were you when your teacher/lecturer just droned out facts and figures?

I know, from personal experience, this doesn't stick in your mind. I took a Computing A-Level at College.

Now it has to be said, I'm a reasonable fan of technology; growing up I was hugely into every bit of technology I could get my hands on.

I knew how circuit boards worked, I even made my own sound card for a computer that worked through the parallel port. (Don't know what I'm talking about? Don't worry, just take me at my word that I was geeky).

Yet I got an E in Computing.

An *E* for goodness sake.

I had come out of School with an A* in GCSE IT, yet got an E in Computing.

And I was a geek.

How did this happen?

Well I can tell you, when I went to University, I had a lecturer who had a *completely* different teaching style. He was far more engaging, and you could say, perhaps in that one year I had matured a touch, but I took an exam in a module that was effectively exactly the same as the

Computing A level I had essentially failed. (We're talking primarily Binary Maths here, if you're interested).

I got over 90% on the paper.

The same applied with Maths for me, actually. I was struggling at GCSE.

My Maths, English and French were terrible; these were considered (obviously) as important subjects by the school I was in, and they insisted on removing me from German to give me extra lessons in Maths/English/French.

Now at the time, I hated them.

I suspect this actually festered a little over the years and I *really* disliked the school for it.

But obviously, they knew what they were doing.

I got given extra maths lessons with a different teacher, who again, had a *completely* different teaching style. He was more friendly, and interwove stories into his lessons.

The result? I went from failing Maths to getting a "higher" B. (The "higher" being the harder paper at the time, or something).

This is because, our minds are hardwired to respond to story. This is exactly why no-one wants to hear about the facts/figures about your product. *They just don't care.*

But tell them about the time you did X when you were growing up, or you did Y last week and it was hilarious - they'll be far more engaged... and you just build in the sale at the end.

The Format (Geeky Stuff)

OK so we've got to cover the geeky stuff. *Don't* overlook this part, it's *really* important.

Right, so first of all, Serif fonts are best used for all offline communication and Sans Serif are thought to be better for online – our most commonly used font is Arial.

But one of the most critical points which I haven't mentioned about Email marketing yet, is that you absolutely must not write your emails in any other format other than normal text, (and I don't quite mean "plain text" as in no HTML) – it's good to be able to choose a nicer font than the 'system' font – but don't go for anything non-standard.

Before You Switch Off: This really is critical and you must understand it.

So... The email that lands in their inbox. It *must* look like it's naturally written (plain text). This means you want to strip out any extra HTML or rubbish from the template, so that there's no logo or borders, or anything fancy.

How you do that is *usually* reasonably simple although it can be a pain in the backside. Ontraport, from memory, is really good for this. Infusionsoft, is terrible (sorry guys, although in fairness I've logged multiple cases over this).

With Infusionsoft, the only way I have found to remove the HTML "padding" they force upon you, is to use their HTML builder. If you've never seen HTML before, you might need a bit of technical help, but essentially you just want to make sure that the code is removed up to the point where you've got

Hi ~Contact.FirstName~

(or similar, obviously). My point here is this: if your emails land in the wrong format, or look wrong, they won't get read in the way that they should be.

But everyone else is doing it...

So why shouldn't you put your logo at the top? Or make the newsletter look attractive? Surely that's what the big companies do and so it must work?

I hear this a lot.

Especially from eCommerce companies.

But the thing is, it works for the bigger Companies because they send out millions of emails every day. I can assure you that the type of email marketing that works more effectively than any other type, is you just writing an email as if you were writing to them from your normal email program.

Think about how many emails you get in your inbox every day.

You might only get a few but you might also get hundreds. I personally get around 300 a day, and every email that contains graphics in the middle of the email, nicely formatted (but missing massive chunks because I haven't downloaded images), is instantly regarded as a newsletter/commercial/junk email.

By approaching the reader with text, you write to them in the format they are expecting to be written to in. This means that your message is far, far more likely to be read – if not, at least scanned very quickly, so if you make the text effective enough you'll capture their attention, and that's all you need to do.

What's the Frequency, Kenneth?

An interesting story behind that question; in this instance I'm referring to the song by REM in the early 90's. I was listening to that track again recently... and for me it brings back all sorts of memories of our early family home.

Memories of, despite being the youngest brother, being the best "at computers" in our family. Having huge aspirations of becoming an "IT Man" from an early age (my love for IT has since faded a little - swapping out CPUs and fixing fans isn't as fun as it used to be).

It's funny how music can trigger such fond memories, this one in particular because it was on a cassette tape (ahh cassette tape... you know I had an apprentice who had no idea what that was... shocking).

This cassette tape got played a lot; normally when I was playing on or fixing our 'family' computer (which in the end was more classified as 'my' computer).

But bringing this back to Email Marketing: it's frequency that most business owners get wrong, because almost always they choose close to zero.

I'm not just talking about Email Marketing, but also how often you pick up the phone, write them a letter or arrange to meet up face to face.

Practically speaking, the majority of those things (especially for the larger customer base) is just not feasible. Meeting face to face for example, wouldn't be practical for an eCommerce Business Owner who sold thousands of products all over the UK.

Telephone calls can be expensive (although lucrative...).

The best way to manage a constant stream of communication is with Email. And the best frequency? Well, I can pretty much promise you that whatever you're doing at the moment, isn't enough!

But here's something really important: if you haven't emailed your clients ever, and you suddenly start emailing them every day, they're going to wonder what the hell's going on. You have to ease into it.

If you've got this big database of clients and you haven't emailed them in ages, the best thing to do, is send them a single email reminding them you exist.

If you start emailing on a relatively regular basis, you position yourself as regularly communicating to your clients. This in turn allows you to send more frequently.

You should be sending *at least* 1 to 2 emails a week.

It's OK If People Tell You To Go Away

You could get offended / take it personally every time someone unsubscribes. But - and this is what I do to be honest - you could also just quite simply not pay any attention to it, whatsoever.

98

Regardless of this though, you **absolutely must** send out emails using a system that will allow unsubscribes and that will monitor 'hard bounces' (i.e. email doesn't exist anymore).

One you've sent out that first emailing, (at which point you should be mentioning you'll be staying in touch more), you could probably start to email fortnightly. Once you've been emailing fortnightly for a while, you could move to weekly. Once you've been emailing weekly for a while, you could move to two a week, then three a week, then every day.

If you think people will get annoyed with your emails – look at it this way: they've got an unsubscribe button.

If they unsubscribe, they were never going to buy from you anyway.

There's No Way I Could Email Every Day, Are You Crazy!?

Yes, probably, just a little bit.

But am I crazy for emailing out every day? No.

I had a reply from someone the other day that summed up for me exactly why I email every day.

Hi Ben...

I have to admit I don't always read your e-mails, some times I don't even open them... but every now and then I actually sit and read... Mostly it makes me think, some times I come away convinced that I'm still heading in the right direction... Phewww... and every now and then I just enjoy the time off to read what happening with you

*... so keep up the good words and hope the book gets
done soon*
Mark

I often get replies along those lines, although very
often they also include an enquiry for doing some
business. That is, if they haven't followed the call to
action.

But it very much describes the reality of the situation.
By emailing frequently and being entertaining and
engaging, you're constantly in peoples minds. So when
they finally decide to make that purchase, whether it be
for a Website or a Takeaway Dinner, you're the one they
think of.

I don't know what to write...

The thing is, it's like most things. The more you do it,
the more proficient you get at it.

I wouldn't say I was a 'natural writer'. Back, many
(many) years ago, I was able to waffle on in things like
course work for School/University, but there's a
difference between waffle content and concise engaging
content that drives a call to action.

This has been learned only by reading guides, books
and more.

What's the biggest turn off when it comes to Emails?
Yep - it's crazy boring.

It's filled with facts, figures and charts and every
statistic under the sun. But no-one really wants to read
all that do they?

Why do people do it? Well, because they think, (and they don't think this because they're stupid, they think this because this is what people have always told them to do) the best way to write about a product is to list every feature it's got.

Whilst I'm sure that one of the best features of the Buggy 2000 is that it's got "Ergonomic Foam handles" I'm not sure I really care.

Maybe if you said "This buggy will be easier and more comfortable to hold with these ergonomic foam handles" I might be slightly more interested/captivated.

My point is, don't just list features and copy specifications or product guides. If you were in a shop or marketplace or wherever you sell, and you were talking to someone selling to them face to face (or over the phone...) - what would you say?

You probably don't realise some of the best sales copy you could ever write comes out of your mouth on a daily basis.

In fact, even better than that, if you're telling friends/family about your product/service, how would you describe what you do, to them?

So when it comes to your regular (whether that's fortnightly, weekly, or daily) emails, write your emails like you're talking to a friend in the pub...

Things like perfect grammar and English are less relevant (but not entirely irrelevant, in fact regular sloppy mistakes make you look pretty unprofessional) but you want to formulate your email like you're talking to that person.

Because you are.

You're talking directly to the reader; you're not talking to a list.

Let me say that again, because that's *so, so important.*

You're talking directly to the reader; you're not talking to a list.

Where Do You Get The Time?!

This is something I hear a lot.

The thing is, the physical writing of my daily emails takes around 20 minutes, *generally.* Sometimes it can take longer, and sometimes I'll write 2 or 3 in one go if it's a particularly big story.

When you start out, it might take an hour. It will feel forced, but that's ok. Run with it.

Over time, this will get easier and easier. And in fact you'll find that things will crop up during the day, or you'll think of something whilst in the shower, and you'll chuckle to yourself and say "that'll make a great daily email".

I frequently pull stories out of my head that come from childhood, and it's very often they can quite easily tie into what I'm selling, but if not - you just end it with "and whilst I'm here I must remind you to get this gadget...".

To prove the point, here's a complete example of one of my daily emails:

Hi Ben,

I wouldn't say I was a particularly rebellious child growing up. I adhered to the rules pretty much at school.

I was lucky in that I went to a 'decent school'. Having passed my 11+ I was inline to follow my brothers to a Grammar School in our area. I have to admit I don't know that I enjoyed all of it, but then who does?!

Anyway... I'm pretty sure this was in Year 9, because I'm sure my "Partner in Crime" was Year 11 and I know I was 2 years younger than him... So that would make me around 13-14.

This wasn't Steve though...I don't think he was involved..(but he might have been, this is going back a fair bit...). This was someone else, equally geeky as I recall. He must have been because I'm pretty sure he wrote most of the program, although I know I had my fair share of input.

For any fellow geeks on the list, bear with me if things seem simplified, but I'm aware not everyone will care about the technical details....

So what did we do? Well, being young teenagers keen to "rebel" in our own way (the geeky way) we thought we'd have a go at the "IT manager"...(if you could call him that....). He was always deleting our copies of games we had carefully hidden... rather rude if you ask me... Anyway, we had observed, in our own awesome way, that every time the PC booted it erased all the data from "T drive" - a shared network drive that was effectively on the server.

Wouldn't it be funny to put something on that drive that meant it would take ages to reboot?? (Well, to a geeky teenager then, the answer is Yes. I appreciate the answer might be "Why?" now...). But that wasn't taking it far enough... no... We'd determined the best way to cause havoc, would be to create loads of data on each PC then reboot them all it would take ages to boot up to Windows. Hilarious I tell you...

So how did we do it? Well, we wrote a program to do it. We did it in a VERY simple coding language intended to teach us the basics of programming, and basically made it create a folder on the drive with random characters and letters. Doesn't sound too complex no? Well, the funny bit is, because we used random special characters, Windows wasn't able to delete them. We knew the techie would probably have a little bit of trouble with that...

In order to not get caught (clearly an important factor here) we decided to run the program under 1st Years logins. How did we guess those? Easy. Go to the sports board, find all the kids in the football club (you KNOW they wouldn't have reset their password) and go login with their initial and last name, and password of "password".

It worked like a dream. On our last count we'd created over a million folders on each PC. We rebooted all PCs and went off innocently to our lessons. It worked maybe a little too well though. It didn't just slow them down, it totally broke them. Nothing worked, at all. Dead. Oops...

On a break a little while later, I was with said partner in crime. We were going to go to the computer room, but, well it was down (how inconsiderate of someone?!) so we went to the technology block, as the PCs there weren't linked to the main network.

On our way through the main door (and this noise echo'ing around the school entrance will last with me forever):

"WATERS!! (and someone else here)"

(I've removed the name of the other person... but that's the other guy I did this with...). I don't ever recall seeing this teacher (the head of IT...with the "IT Manager" sat next to him...) angry, either before or since this occasion.

Ah. Something wrong sir?

We had performed I guess what you could really refer to as a School boy error...We had run the program under the 1st years accounts so untraceable, but oops, we'd left the original source code in our own home directories.

Sigh.

Needless to say, there was (well deserved) punishment, Saturday detention amongst other things...plus we had to write the antidote (which really wasn't hard, but I feel that was more of a point of principle).

We had a lot of fun with that School Network / Computer system...and the story of the Technology Block Computer Room must be saved for another day...

...no real sales message here, just an amusing story. **Last chance to book my final slot for a meeting on Monday by the way***...remember, your competition will almost definitely have given up for the year now - so don't hang around, make 2014 a great year and do it on the back of a solid marketing campaign!*

Kind regards

Ben

PS. After the initial meeting with the teacher we were sent off to the headmaster. We were made to feel very sorry for what we'd done. Funny though, if it was me in his shoes, I'd do the opposite. If they'd recognised we'd actually achieved something pretty cool at the age of 14/16 and harnessed on to that with encouragement/stronger IT focus (this was the mid 90's so hardly likely) who knows where our programming skills would have ended up.... anyway, have a great weekend (after you book this meeting)!

The highlighted bold sections were links; and as you can see, I was simply engineering face to face meetings, and my story had nothing to do with that.

That was from quite some time ago, and I can't remember the *exact* response of that one email, but I know the emails I sent within that 2-3 week period on the run up to Christmas generated me quite a few meetings!

In terms of *time* - that Email took perhaps 20-30 minutes to write, because I was simply writing of a memory, something that happened to me. And when you're effectively telling a story of something that happened to you - the words can flow quite easily. Sure it's not grammatically perfect, but that doesn't matter.

If they don't, there's one trick.

It relates to "write as you speak" - and that's to effectively talk to a Dictaphone or similar (use a voice memo app on your phone - perhaps). Talk about the memory or story you have.

Once you're done - simply write it up!

CHAPTER EIGHT

Social Media

It's all about the Likes and Shares, right?

Many people that I talk to are under the impression that if you don't take hold of Social Media in your business, you're losing out on huge profits and your competitors will win your potential business.

Other people that I talk to are under the impression Social Media is a complete waste of time, and are only interested in other strategies like Google or Direct Mail / Print Advertising etc.

So who's right?

Well, the answer is, neither and both. It's not possible to generalise Social Media on an overall basis, because the facilities and markets open to each Social Media platform vary.

For example, advertising on Facebook might bring you awesome results, advertising on another platform, no results. Doing the exact same thing for the business next door in the exact same way, may give you the exact opposite.

I tend to summarise Social Media in the following way:

• It doesn't matter if you have 100 fans, or 100,000 fans on Facebook. It doesn't matter if you have 25,000 followers on Twitter. This is not going to bring you a *predictable* or *scalable* stream of customers. That's not to say you can't utilise a big fanbase - but it's not where I'd focus your energy initially.

• It's rarer than you think to have content that "goes viral". To force this to happen takes a **huge** amount of work and investment, and the ROI is extremely difficult to gauge.

• Making 100 tweets a day about your business will *probably* get you nowhere. Tweeting to people about how you can help them or some other reason to get them to opt in to your system *may* bring you further traffic – but has to be done in a careful and controlled way, otherwise you're just reported for spamming them.

The other question that I'm regularly asked is, "What Social Networks should we be bothered with?"
This is an interesting question and largely depends on your industry and market. For example – you might think it's no good if you're selling consumer products to advertise them on LinkedIn.
You might get some response or even a few sales, but you're not going to be hitting the right market... or you might hit exactly the right market and you get more sales than if you advertised all day long on Facebook.

Test & Measure.
Test & Measure.
Test & Measure.

For the sake of simplicity, I'll split out the following sections to differentiate between consumer/business.

Business To Consumer

I would primarily recommend focusing on Facebook, although Twitter and Instagram are your other obvious platforms and I market on all of them for many clients. The thing is, and this ties back into Pay Per Click, Facebook is really the best because of the capablities of the targeting and the promoted posts (which in turn essentially means we're doing pay per click).

In either case, whether it be Facebook, Twitter or Instagram, the key to success, much like with the Facebook Pay Per Click, is to get people *off* social media. I regularly run competitions for our clients, but the rules dictate that the user must sign up with their name/email into a list. Thus, we have their details elsewhere and can regularly re-market to them.

But still, platforms like Facebook - and even Twitter to a degree - have very special and carefully written algorithms in place. These mean that they only show the posts you make, to people they think want to see them.

This might be really frustrating to you as a business user on Facebook, but as a consumer, this is awesome.

Some people moan, but they don't really realise what their news feed would look like if they saw every post made by every page/person. For many it'd just flood their feed and they'd miss valued posts.

So how can you make sure your posts *are* seen by the right people?

OK... Now we're asking the right question. Well, my honest answer kind of comes back to Pay Per Click. But not in the sense of setting up targeted Ads, etc... No, instead, what you can do is create a post on a regular basis (whether that be daily, weekly, fortnightly or even monthly) and then promote it.

You promote it to the people who like your page (and possibly their friends, depends on what you're selling) but if that's not entirely appropriate, you can promote to a pre-defined audience.

This can be the same as your main PPC audience, obviously, meaning you can keep both your organic and your PPC audiences catered for.

The only disadvantage of this is you can't clearly define which is PPC traffic and which is organic... but if you're only putting in a few £ here and there, it saves time and a lot of effort.

Business To Business

In terms of communicating to your customers, the most obvious platform is LinkedIn.

LinkedIn gives you the opportunity of connecting with people you've met very briefly (i.e. potential clients) and people that you're planning to meet. It's a great tool because you can arm yourself with a little bit more information before you meet them. Although if you don't want them to know you've been looking at their profile, you might want to pay to go Premium, then change your settings so that people only see "a person in X industry".

So why bother connecting to people on LinkedIn?

Being part of a professional network opens you up to communicating with potential customers more often. I have to confess I don't hold a *massive* value over it, and I wouldn't put any primary focus or efforts into building your connections.

But, as an example, if you have visited a client and connected to them on LinkedIn, you can send them a direct message to follow up on your meeting.

Your connections will build naturally over time – and it should be a tool that helps build on potential business, rather than being a tool to try and generate it - unless we're talking Pay Per Click to your website, and I covered that in the Pay Per Click section.

There are a few "obvious" things to both look at and talk about when it comes to LinkedIn. The most obvious is your profile page; have a look at it from an "External" point of view.

Isn't it boring? Have you just got your title as your job title? (Probably says "Director" or something else equally snoozeworthy).

Liven up your profile, and start treating it like any other direct response marketing piece. Create a desire for action; provide a call to action - whether that be to call you, to connect with you or to visit a web page.

Whatever your call to action - make sure it stands out and your LinkedIn profile will continue to bring you more leads.

Although that's assuming you actually do something with LinkedIn. So that means accepting and generating connection requests.

Remember, when someone connects with you - drop them a quick thankyou and see if you can help each other. You'll find that you're getting an awful lot more out of your Social Media if you start doing this.

CHAPTER NINE
Video Marketing

Why Use Video Marketing?

It's important to remember, when considering types of Marketing strategies, not to base them only on what *you* do.

Now it's important to target the right Market, and that might mean targeting someone *like you* - but that's not to say they'll have the same behavioural traits as you.

i.e. You might never click on an Advert, but they do. You might never watch videos online, they might only watch videos online.

It's interesting actually, a while ago I decided to make chocolate. I thought it'd be a really fun thing to do with the kids; you know, roast the beans, grind them up and make this chocolate from scratch.

Obviously, I was mistaken...

Where did it all start? Well, I saw an advert on TV for a chocolate bar maker. It looked cool. I found it on Amazon for next day delivery. I bought it.

(A clear case of advertising working right?)

But I didn't stop there. I found some raw Cacao beans and bought them too.

When we were ready to give it a go, I jumped on to Google and found a load of websites telling me how to make chocolate.

Virtually *all* the Websites I found, seemed to be a video tutorial.

I was getting annoyed, because I was on my phone. I'm used to step by step text tutorials, and whilst I don't mind watching the odd video on my phone, I was trying to cook in the kitchen - it just wasn't going to happen.

In the end I gave in and I took the iPad out with me, and for the first time watched video guides as I cooked.

But then it occurred to me... millions of people will be doing this every day. Googling some sort of recipe, and watching it in their kitchen. (OK, I'm not *that* stupid, it didn't *just* occur to me but I hadn't experienced it truly first hand until then).

But the other thing is, on quite a few of these videos I watched, they had Ads on the start. Some I watched, some I didn't.

And regardless of whether you're on YouTube, or embedding video in your Blog, millions of people watch these videos every day.

You can target your market in much the same way you can with normal Google ads. So... Why wouldn't you record a marketing video that spoke to these people?

Video marketing is often overlooked...

Video marketing is often overlooked or considered annoying, or it's not effective when it's done.

The reason for this is, that like website copy, the majority of videos will talk about how "we have been in business 25 years" or "we do the best job around". It might be that you do the best job because you have been around 25 years, but realistically, why does the customer care. All the customer wants to hear is what's in it for them, why should they be interested in this product, how will it help them?

With that being said, there are four main ways for you to record a video for your website:

1.   You talking to the camera
2.   A professional talking to the camera
3.   You (or a professional) doing a voiceover on Power Point style presentation
4.   Animation

You Talking To The Camera

Many people are worried about being on camera, not looking the best / most professional. But, here's the thing – anyone viewing that will instantly start to get a feel for who you are, and will start to build that connection with you. It's like you giving a personal sales pitch to every single person that visits your website.

This has the benefit that it's very low cost to do (I'm not saying you have to shoot it using your camera phone, but compared to the alternatives this is one of the lowest cost options – in fact I record all my marketing videos on my iPhone with an external mic now).

It might be that you're worried about this looking amateurish and that this might turn people away; if this is the case, talk to some production companies near you.

One of the things they will do is help you put together a script, coach you through talking to the camera, professionally shoot it and edit it to make sure it's as professional as could be.

This latter option is great if you're really looking to "outsource" the production as much as possible, but are keen to be behind the camera.

A Professional Talking to The Camera

If you really don't want to go on camera, even with a production company talking you through it, then you can look at hiring a professional to do the talking for you.

The benefits of this solution include the fact that you can write down bullet points that you want your message to include, and the production company can put together a script for the trained spokesperson, who can then face the camera and talk for you.

The negatives of this solution include the fact that the cost is higher, and depending on your target market the video may be perceived differently before it's had a chance to deliver its message. What I mean by that, is by the potential customer seeing the video in a more 'non-professional' environment, they're transported into the room with you, listening to the message from you.

When it's a completely professional video, it becomes more like a sales pitch. So you've got to be careful, and be extra sure the message you deliver conveys the benefit – not the features (we'll cover this more in the next chapter).

You (or a professional) doing a voiceover on Power Point

style presentation

This option is another great low cost one, and if you're really against being on camera, this can be another way of you delivering a personal message without having to be in front of the camera.

If you have PowerPoint, and have used it before, then this will become even easier to produce very quickly. You can put your slideshow together, and then use PowerPoint to record a voiceover. You could potentially have a video done in the next 30 minutes.

Again because this option doesn't have you facing the camera, building that personal connection – you have to make sure that the first few seconds are really capturing the viewer's attention.

Animation

When done properly, this option works really well. The reason being it can be very attention-grabbing and entertaining from the outset.

However, it can also be the most expensive to implement. These sorts of videos are very time consuming, and to get that "right image" it can take some skilled hands – which often come at a higher price.

You can combine animation and video as well, which can provide a very effective combination of grabbing the attention of the user whilst building that personal connection.

As with all the video options, you have to remember to convey the message that gives the viewer a reason to want to talk to you further. It doesn't matter how great your product or service is – without some reason that they need the product or service, it's irrelevant.

Where To Advertise The Video

Once you've got your video created, where do you publish it?

On your Website? On your Homepage? This is often the biggest mistake people make. They'll go to all the effort of getting a video produced, but then do nothing with it.

It's much like spending £5,000 on a website, then doing *no* marketing for it at all.

So there are a couple of options open to you, apart from anywhere on your website or your homepage.

Firstly, I'd look at embedding it inside your Landing Page. Now, this page might want to be entirely focused on the video, or it might just be a small part of it.

I tend to focus primarily on the video, but have enough copy on the landing page so that you can do either or. Not everyone has speakers/headphones, and not everyone wants to watch a video.

The other place to advertise is YouTube.

YouTube advertising is great, because like Pay Per Click, you're generally only paying when people are watching the Ad. i.e. there's an option to skip the Ad. This means combined with some targeting, and an initial engaging first 5 seconds (the amount of time they're "forced" to watch the Ad) you can get great returns from YouTube.

Although as with Facebook, you've got to get them *off* YouTube as quickly as possible, because they're almost certainly watching funny videos of cats, and won't be in the mood to be sold to.

CHAPTER TEN

Search Engine Optimisation (The Truth)

If I do XYZ I'll get a ton of free traffic

OK so let's forget the term "free traffic". SEO is *not* free traffic.

Don't get me wrong, if you're getting a load of visits as a result of SEO, and that's leading to a load of business, great.

But that's a *bonus*. You shouldn't, and in fact, must not rely on it, and you certainly shouldn't be spending huge amounts of money to get you into or maintain, a position.

The other thing to note here is, that it doesn't allow for serious amounts of testing & measuring, but I'll come back to that in a minute.

I can think of two businesses local to me who were very dependant on Google organic traffic.

In fact without it, their business would fold – they were always very cautious over changing anything that might affect how Google ranked them.

But, the thing is, you don't have to change anything.

Google is changing things all the time. Google is always trying to improve its algorithm and how it ranks websites.

Those companies that I have seen, suffered from this fate.

Google rolled out an update and their rankings dropped tens of pages. Within months both had closed.

There is no reason this couldn't happen to you if you're completely dependent on Google organic traffic.

It's not free

So here's the thing.

SEO (unless you got lucky with some content, which leads me more on to the "don't rely on it" bit later), is not free.

It might be free at point of delivery, and the best example I can think of here is the NHS, but it's not free from cost.

Whether it's your time in writing blogs, content, or paying a company to do that, it all costs. And if you take the attitude that "your time is free" because you're doing it in the evening or weekend, don't.

Because if you put that time into something more productive, that's going to directly result in generating a lead or enquiry, you're going to get a lot more sales, a lot faster.

Depend On It And Risk It All

It's one thing to reap the rewards of some SEO.

OK, you paid some guy £5000 to get you to number one, but it's ok, you only pay him £500 a month now but you're generating £10,000 a month in sales.

All from SEO.

Sounds amazing doesn't it…. and it is. I can't deny that spending £500 for a return of £10,000 is crazy good. But like I said, don't depend on it.

Because if you become dependent on Google Organic traffic as an income stream for your business, you're risking it all.

Sound melodramatic?

The thing is… Google don't really want you paying someone £500 to do "SEO".

They don't like it because they want their own algorithm to do all the hard work, because they want it done honestly.

So, Google are continually working on finding ways to negatively impact what you're doing, to positively impact your website positioning.

Not because they don't like you, but because they don't like what you're doing.

Google want relevance.

This is the same with PPC, the higher the relevance the better it performs…

What I'm really saying is, if your SEO is a direct result of links you've effectively paid for, Google want to find a way to negate their relevance.

And they're good at doing it, too. I have personally witnessed a hugely popular Website go from Page 1 to

70, subsequently destroying the business. All from an algorithm update.

Testing & Measuring

So if you do Pay Per Click properly, and you've read/absorbed how that all works, you'll know one of the biggest keys to its success is Split Testing.

Because you need to test & measure.

With Pay Per Click, you can split test your Ads, and split test your landing pages.

So you can continually make them better, and better, and better.

Something that delivers you leads at £50 per lead in Month 1, could be delivering you leads for £45 by Month 3.

That doesn't sound like a huge improvement, but if your budget is £500 per month, that's an extra lead for just optimising a page.

By Month 6 it could be £40, or lower.

The great thing with Pay Per Click, is that it's guaranteed traffic. You don't have to worry about an algorithm update putting you from Page 1 to Page 70.

And it's scaleable.

So if your budget is £500 and you're getting 10 leads, if there's enough search for it, you can put your budget to £5000 and get 100 leads.

But you can't do any of this with SEO.

You can't, one month, say to your SEO guy "hey, if I pay you £5000 this month instead of £500, can I get 10x the traffic please?".

You might get 10x the traffic over time, but it's not scaleable in the same way Pay Per Click is.

CHAPTER ELEVEN

Advertising Offline

We've all been there.

As business owners, I think it's fair to say - we've all "been there". The phone rings, and it's Steve from the local newspaper, magazine or some other popular advertising company. They have a "one off" offer that if you run the ad today you'll save £250 and it'll be seen by 50,000 people. But wait, to get the most effectiveness, you need to run at least 3 ads, if not 5 because it takes a while for it to sink in before people phone you...

Well, after the first 5 minutes you were sceptical but after an hour of talking to Steve you're thinking this all sounds great, so you pay, run the ad and wait for the phones to ring. Because over 50,000 people will see your Ad.

After all, 5 Ads at £250 each, that's just £1250, and if 50,000 people are seeing it, and just 0.1% pick up the phone that's 50 people. If just 10% of that 0.1% bought from you, considering the gadget you're selling is £500, you'll have made £2,500.

And you're sure to get more than that, right? That's just the *worst case figures.* Right?!

But... the phones don't ring. Tumbleweed rolls by as you wait for the phone to ring. In fact, yep, you, along with a huge percentage of other businesses, have just been screwed by one of the most deadly approaches to advertising. Going for the medium first, *then* working out the message and not even focusing on the market at all.

Look at it this way - **you** should know your target market. Do you actually *care* how many people read your ad, really? (The answer is no. If you answered yes, think again.)

Look at it this way: The phones aren't ringing... and 0.1% is a tiny conversion rate, so why aren't people interested?

Well it's easy to compare - if you were selling high quality organic prime beef burgers, would you advertise them in a vegetarian recipe magazine? No, that would be crazy and stupid. But to an extent if you take the approach above, that's pretty much what's happening.

So how do you target your advertising properly? Well, the first answer to that is consider your market before your medium. If you're called with an Advert space for a great newspaper, question this first: are the people I want to reach going to be reading that?

Following on from that it's simple... Focus on the 3 M's and you'll be on your way. Remember, don't always advertise your product in the same magazine as your competitors just because you think that's the right place.

Test and measure, but if you're selling yachts, why not try a golfing magazine or similar? Think of your target market, then work out where they might be, then work out your message!

Direct Mail

So why Direct Mail? What form of Direct Mail works best? How do you go about it? Does the paper quality matter?

So many questions.

What I'll share with you here is based on my actual experience of Direct Mail, alongside a ton of information I've read and absorbed from leading experts in marketing.

The most important part of what I have just said though, is that I'm sharing this stuff based on actual things I've done. Because for Direct Mail to work you *actually have to send* the letters.

It's expensive, right?

So many business owners completely dismiss Direct Mail these days. It's shocking, but understandable.

After all, if you can buy a database of 500,000 people for £350 and someone will SPAM them for £250 why would you spend £600 to send out a letter to 500 people?

If you think the former is acceptable you have a bigger problem.

You should only **ever** send Email to people that have directly opted-in to receive it.

For two reasons. Firstly, because Email is treated very differently to post, psychologically speaking. People are 'always on' with Email, and we all get a lot of really rubbish SPAM, so unless they've specifically asked for an Email from you, you shouldn't send it. Secondly, because it can damage you for legitimate Email marketing.

Another plain good reason for Direct Mail is because people are busy... and going back to the 'always on' attitude with Email it's quite easy to miss an email (maybe your email landed right whilst they were talking to an important customer on the phone, and they clicked on it, off it, then never went back to it).

Even if they're getting regular Email Marketing from you, they can go through 3-4 emails without really reading them. But when they get a letter through the post, it's pretty unlikely they won't even open it.

From a cost point of view, you shouldn't look at a campaign as a total cost anyway. You should be looking at it as a cost per lead or cost per customer. And as long as that cost per customer is lower than your lifetime value of that customer, you're doing well.

What Works Best

Well, that's a very broad question which is very specific to your industry, your product or service, and where you are in your sales process.

One effective way to send the initial direct mail when you're really early in the relationship is to send using a postcard.

Postcards get a high readership simply because they don't need opening. There are quite a few sites out there that will provide the data as well as the print and send service – the benefit of that is you can design your postcard, work out who you want to send it to by area, then send out a mailshot. Or, you can upload a CSV of your customers/leads you want to send it to, and then they will print and send it for you.

This is a great tool to promote an event or a specific call to action; if you're trying to encourage users to perhaps obtain a free copy of your report or guide, this is a great way to do it. Once they've made that interaction, that expression of interest, you know you can build your own list of who to re-market to.

Remember, the same rules apply here when it comes to engaging the reader. Make sure your headline isn't trying to sell something.

You want to attract attention to their problem, and how you can solve it.

What does your product do that makes their life easier?

Try to put yourself in their shoes – what is it that makes your product / service better than anyone else's?

What is it that makes *you* the person to go to, and not your competitor who's actually next door to them?

Remember, even if you're giving something away for free – you still have to sell it.

You still have to convince them that whatever it is you want them to do, it's worth doing – that they would be making a huge mistake if they didn't.

Once you've started this process, you can refine your postcard format and send it out, area by area, testing the results each time.

Remember, they don't have to go to your website, they can go to "free-internet-marketing-guide.com" (ok that one's a little bit long – but the message is in the domain name itself).

It's often better, if you can, to set up a domain name that's relevant to the product/service/guide you're promoting.

Not only does it allow for campaign-specific performance statistics, but it's relevant and more memorable for the reader too.

CHAPTER TWELVE

Build a relationship, not a sale

How soon should you sell to someone?

So, how soon should you sell to someone?

Well, that depends.

If someone has typed in to Google "buy gadget model ABCZ1" then take them to a page to sell them that gadget. But that's one of the few times I'd take someone to a direct sales page.

You might think, "I only sell sellotape, how can I build a relationship?"

It doesn't matter what your industry is, what you provide or how you provide it. You can always offer advice to people around what you sell, or around the problem that what you sell solves.

Think about a guide "The 10 types of sellotape you didn't know existed for all kinds of tasks".

I would say the biggest myth flying around, and the one that retailers fall for all the time, is people use the Internet to buy.

Yes – people *do buy* on the Internet, but that's not what they *primarily* use it for.

You might be thinking "Don't be crazy, I buy online all the time!" – but think very carefully about your day, from morning to evening.

How much time do you spend reading the news? On Facebook? On a forum or maybe a hobby related website? How often do you think "I think I'll buy one of those" – then Google it to find out more information...

My point is – conversion rates wouldn't be so low on an industry average if more people solely used the Internet to buy – but the fact is, people want more information on something they are often *considering* purchasing.

You might be searching around online to compare prices for something you're about to buy in the high street, or be searching around online for the best deal. This can tie in with 'bundling' other products with the main product to make the initial product look like it has a better offer.

So, how do we make use of this traffic?

What's the point?

If they're coming to your site to find out a bit of information what can we do? How can we take a conversion rate from 2% up to 20%?

Building "Opt Ins"

One of the best ways to start a relationship online is to give something away, and if people are looking for information, why not give it to them?

I don't tend to recommend giving part of your service or product away like a free trial, as that can devalue your product/service.

But giving a free report or guide is a great way to start a relationship, and far more effective than the typical common tactic to try and extract personal details in the form of "join our newsletter".

Think of the number of sites you see which have "Join our newsletter for updates".

Who cares?

Really?

If you're constantly expanding your products and services then you could look at offering an update on "upcoming new products which will solve your problem of X by doing Y" – but this still isn't enough generally to convince (enough) people to give you their personal details.

And by that I mean to make the Pay Per Click cost effective.

Because we're doing this, through Pay Per Click, right? Right.

People hate junk email / spam, and hate being harassed.

Quite often, if they will fill out a form online, that's exactly what they expect will happen – they will be harassed. So how do we handle this?

This will, of course, vary completely depending on what you do, but take a few examples:

Travel Agent: Download our free guide on 'How to get the most out of Orlando'

Estate Agent: Download our free guide on 'How to get the maximum price for your property'

E-commerce: Download our guide on 'How to make the right Rug choice for your room'

There are hundreds of different opportunities no matter what your market and no matter what you're selling. A free information guide is great, and if you can, look at getting some printed.

It only needs to be a few pages, and these can be produced at really low cost. You could produce them in-house to trial it initially, but I'd recommend getting them done professionally – this will be the first thing your potential customer gets from you, so you want to make sure it's the right quality.

Also, if you send it out in the post, rather than as a downloadable PDF – you're increasing the likelihood it will actually be read. You'll decrease your initial conversion rate, because people will have to give you their address, but in the long run, the physical address is far more valuable. You then have their address - so you're able to co-ordinate your online marketing with some direct mail.

The thing is because so many people offer downloads here and there, your download will be lost within their 'downloads folder' or desktop. If you have a booklet on their desk, or at home, it sits much more in their focus.

Don't just be sending sales letters or trying to sell through the post. The aim of this process is to build a long term relationship where the potential customer sees you as a source of information – an authority on your subject.

Going back to the 'Newsletter' idea, this is rubbish for Email but works quite well for Direct Mail. You can incorporate special offers, but also bring a complete personal touch.

How many of your competitors would send 2-3 pages of written content along with just one special offer for a product?

It used to be that years ago, you would look at 7 points of contact to a sale. You would write a letter, make a telephone call, write a letter, make a telephone call, etc. This process could also take much longer.

Over the last 10 years, our lives have changed so much with the introduction of the Internet in our daily lives, and with the constant flow of sales messages hitting our inboxes all day – this process has grown significantly. You're now looking at up to 28 points of contact or more for a sale. This might seem like an absolutely impossible task, but this will lead really nicely into our next section – Email marketing.

Testimonials

This section is really hugely important for the success of your online campaign. "Social proof" that your product works, reassures people. The trouble is – it's become so common place to have testimonials on your site now, that it becomes questionable as to whether they're trustworthy or not.

If you're Business To Business – then this becomes a slightly easier problem to solve. You can, (usually with the customer's permission!), leave the customer's name and company name alongside the testimonial, making it feel more authentic and also – should the potential customer wish – verifiable.

If you're Business To Consumer – then the only way to truly get around this (and this is great for B2B as well) is to use video testimonials. This is significantly harder to get done – but is less frequently implemented by your competitors – so the more you can source and put on your website the better. Really simple, face to camera style "I bought X and it totally solved my problem Y, and the person Z from the company was brilliant". Five or six of those on your website and your conversions will dramatically increase.

The advantage of having video testimonials is that, as well as embedding them on to your website, you can host them on YouTube, which is of course the world's second biggest search engine.

The benefit of this is that you can include keywords around the problem your product solves, and people can get a first-hand recommendation before they even visit your website.

How many testimonials should you have? Well, as many as possible but how you structure that is important. You don't want people scrolling through pages and pages of recommendations otherwise the call to action loses focus. It's best, if you can, if you can slide through a few different testimonials, but if you've got video then you could group some in between some sales/promotional material (i.e. you could develop a video which talks about your product, combines some animation, and also some customer testimonials).

Just to mention as well, sometimes the word "testimonials" doesn't quite fit with the image you want on your website, which is fine. You can go with Customer Comments, Feedback or even Case Studies.

A strong case study with a customer comment can work wonders for conversion ratios, as people are able to see a full in depth analysis of what you've done, and the fact that the customer is happy.

It's a Marathon, Not a Sprint

The thing to remember with your online marketing, from your website to your adverts, is that you're never finished.

Business owners seem to treat the website as being something that "has to be done". And once it's done, that's it - it's done.

Tick it off the list and move on.

Ah, how wrong you can be.

I have fully replaced our Website at least once a year, and I have made significant changes on average at least once every three months, and we make changes to landing pages sometimes almost weekly.

Around mid 2013, I decided to make a change. A change in my life that would see me 'get fit'.

Actually, I think I made that decision around March/April 2013, when I was watching the London Marathon on TV, but I actually did something about it by Summer.

You see, around 3-4 years previous to that, I'd made an active effort to get fit.

I'd got into a bit of running. I enjoyed it.

Then Josh (our first child) came along and with a combination of work and sleepless nights, the regular runs slipped to, eventually, no runs at all. Over a few years I ended up putting a bit of weight back on, so I decided enough was enough and it's time to get back into running.

Explaining this to a 3 year old was interesting, he couldn't figure out why I needed to. But I explained how if you don't do exercise (like him running around the house like a madman) then your tummy will get big.

I hired a Personal Trainer, with the goal of getting me running. No plans to do anything extreme, but I had to start somewhere: I could only just manage 1-2k.

So I signed up for a local 10k Race.

I had about 3 months to prepare, and prepare I did.

Catherine (my wife), Josh and Zach (our kids) came to cheer me on... and witnessed me absolutely in pieces at the end.

I gave it *everything* I had, and I was shattered.

But, having another goal was important.

When I was losing weight the first time round (before Josh) it was for the London to Southend Bike ride. I'd just got married and I wanted to really focus on changing my life for the better... but I hadn't set any subsequent goals and so I took the easy route when Josh came along: forget the training and sleep instead.

So… The first goal this time was for me to run a 10k run, but I needed a longer term goal; both the London to Southend Bike ride and 10k run were great short term goals.

When you hit your goals early the key is to move the goal posts. Make the goal harder.

So I decided to run the London Marathon. I wanted a guaranteed place (so I had a fixed goal) so I chose a Charity (Anthony Nolan - great charity).

Again, when explaining this to Josh, he found it very confusing why I'd want to run for hours and hours, but then he got distracted by the dog chasing his tail, so it was all good.

A few days later he said something that made me chuckle, but was also something that's a key to success.

"Daddy, why's your tummy still big?"

Cheeky so and so. But, it's not like it disappears overnight. It's hard work, determination and discipline.

Just like with your Business.

The things I'm explaining to you are not magical overnight cures. There is no magic pill that can make your business double its profits overnight.

Optimisation is the only way you can continually, consistently and organically grow your Business.

The First Changes Are The Hardest

Just like with the Marathon training, the changes you need to make at the start are by far the hardest.

Getting up off the sofa and getting out for a 5-10k run, on a regular basis, is hard work when you've been living your life on a sofa.

I read a book, some time ago, that made a big difference to my life.

It was called "Switch: How to change things when change is hard" by Chip Heath.

I can honestly say without that book, I wouldn't have implemented half the things I did in my business - not because I didn't know about them - but because it comes down to more than just knowing, you have to do something to make a difference.

I highly recommend that book, although the overall ethos is carried out throughout much of what I talk about here.

The Elephant And The Rider

So in the book Switch, they reference The Happiness Hypothesis by Jonathan Haidt.

Haidt talks about our emotional side as an Elephant, with the rational side as the Rider.

If you just address the Rider (the rational side), you get acceptance that you *should* be doing something, and you *know* you need to do it, but the motivation is missing.

You don't put your heart into it and subsequently you don't get the right results.

If you just address the Elephant (the emotional side), you get the massive desire to do something, but lack the direction and action provided by the rational side.

By addressing both, you get the change you want.

This really struck a chord with me, and the rest of the book, Switch, really helps reinforce how countless examples prove that if you address the Rider AND the Elephant you get results.

There's a *lot* more to it than that, and I couldn't do it justice here, so I heartily recommend you go and get that book once you've finished this one. It *will* help you when it comes to sticking with the change you need to implement.

Because that's the other thing.

Sticking to it is hard.

Running Out Of Steam

If, like me, you're "Office Based" - your business probably revolves around you sitting at a desk a lot.

I used to be primarily a Developer.

That means that for nearly 10 years of my career, both employed and running my own business I spent my time at a desk, for up to 12-14 hours a day, coding.

I was sitting down, eating junk food, with minimal effort involved for tea/coffee or to get out and get more food.

But I'd end the day exhausted; OK the junk food wouldn't have helped in terms of energy levels – but even if I was eating healthily I'd end the day physically shattered.

And many people failed to understand how exhausting sitting at a desk can be.

You're using serious brain power (assuming you're working hard and have a relatively complex job...of course), and by continually focusing all day long, you're tiring out the Rider.

Subsequently, the Elephant goes where it wants, not where the Rider wants it to go.

So when it came to things like dieting, the will power was absolutely devastated come night fall. Eating healthily never lasted.

The problem here is, implementing change is really hard... because when the Rider is exhausted, and you're not going in the right direction, it feels like a self-fulfilling prophecy.

If I'm honest, off the back of a bit of knowledge (that I'd had for quite some time) and the book Switch, and some serious self discipline, I started to roll out the changes I needed.

And the one decision that completely changed my life was saying out loud "I'm not a developer".

I used to live by digging through the code we were rolling out for clients, almost line by line, picking out little issues and making it "perfect".

But that's not how you grow a business.

So now - I don't even open the development software unless there's a catastrophic issue that needs my personal attention.

Which is pretty rare.

And what did that do? It allowed me to focus on what I needed to focus on.

It allowed me to write this book, too.

It allowed me to grow the business through the implementation of marketing strategies, rather than just knowing I needed to get round to doing a direct mail campaign at some point in the near future (but never getting round to it due to being too "busy").

CHAPTER THIRTEEN
A Final Word

The Worst Thing You Can Do

You know what most Business Owners are guilty of? Finding something that works, and then not doing it again! Once you've got something that works, don't stop.

But crucially, the same applies for when it goes wrong: if you've tried some Pay Per Click and got no results after spending some money – evaluate *why*.

What is stopping people buying or enquiring? Consider everything – but **don't give up**. Pay Per Click *is* the most effective way of getting traffic to your site, it's the way of getting the most relevant traffic to your site, full of people that are ready to buy.

The other secret to success with the implementation of all this is, don't implement one at a time.

"This week we'll try some direct mail, maybe next week we'll try some pay per click".

The problem with this attitude is that all too often, you don't start the next task at all, or even if you do it's after weeks and months.

Consider your business as a building, supported by pillars.

Each pillar is the way in which you obtain customers. If you only have one pillar, your building is at significant risk of falling down if something goes wrong.

If you have 4, 8, 12 or more pillars, your building is stronger and will have more tolerance to one of those pillars falling down. Or two or three.

So the message I'm trying to get across here, is once you've found something that works: don't stop.

Keep doing it. If it's Pay Per Click, scale it up. Slowly start to increase your budgets, and you should find that, once you've established that you can predict the results of the Pay Per Click, you can effectively bring more customers flowing in, as smoothly as turning up a tap.

I understand though, despite everything I write in this book, it's not "as simple as that". In fact it can be a really hard slog running AdWords.

You need help, support and advice on a regular basis. Well, fortunately that's where I can help. As a thankyou for reading my book, I'd like to give you a few further resources that'll help you with your AdWords and online marketing.

I've put together some videos and other goodies for you that'll help you either get stared with Pay Per Click, *or* you're already doing it – will help you get more performance.

To claim them, simply go to:

www.digital-magnetism.co.uk/resources